Structural Forms
in the French Theater
1500–1700

Structural Forms
in the French Theater
1500–1700

by

Darnell Roaten

Philadelphia
UNIVERSITY OF PENNSYLVANIA PRESS

© 1960 by the Trustees of the University of Pennsylvania

Printed in Great Britain, India, and Pakistan
by the Oxford University Press
London, Bombay, and Karachi

Library of Congress Catalogue Card Number: 59-5684

Printed in England at The Curwen Press, Plaistow

To
Robert H. Williams
Teacher, Colleague
and Friend

Preface

As the author always discovers sooner or later, a book on a scholarly subject is inevitably a work of co-operation. It is a privilege to be able to record some of the numerous obligations incurred in the course of writing this essay. Professors Lancaster E. Dabney of the University of Texas, Everett W. Hesse of the University of Wisconsin, and J. Neale Carman of the University of Kansas were kind enough to read the entire manuscript and offer various suggestions for revision. I am specifically indebted to Professor Harold E. Wethey of the University of Michigan for suggestions concerning the illustrations to be used; more generally, he has given help over a period of years in connection with numerous problems in the understanding of the plastic arts. Professor Marian Davis of the University of Texas aided in locating various items of information concerning the illustrations. I am grateful to Professor Robert H. Williams of the University of Texas for reading portions of the manuscript and especially for his steady encouragement during the time when it was being written.

The usual reservation, to the effect that the author alone is responsible for all errors of fact or interpretation, holds good in the case of the work that is herewith presented.

Contents

Illustrations

Structural Forms
in the French Theater
1500–1700

Introduction

There exists a general impression, current among both professional critics and laymen, to the effect that literary criticism constitutes a firmly established discipline with a set of principles that are of unquestioned validity. This opinion probably arose because of the great prestige that has been enjoyed by such works as Aristotle's *Poetics* and Horace's *Ars Poetica*. The precepts which they set forth were reworked in the sixteenth century and were affirmed once more in the eighteenth but no significant innovations were made because the views of the ancients were still regarded as unquestionable dogma. The fact is that literary criticism still has to develop in more than one aspect before it can formulate a doctrine for the most effective understanding of literature as an art. In this respect, literary investigation lags far behind the study of music and the plastic arts, each of which possesses an approach to its critical problems that is widely considered to be capable of solving them. The current study of literature limits itself largely to two activities: (1) gathering factual data concerning such peripheral matters as the establishment of the original text and the unearthing of biographical details about the author; (2) reworking the settled concepts of literary study that have been handed down from such diverse sources as ancient Greece and the nineteenth century. In part, this want of success in originating new theories may be accounted for by the relative youthfulness of criticism as a separate and systematic field of investigation. The study of literature in the modern sense can hardly be said to begin before the eighteenth century. Because of the concentration of the eighteenth-century intellect on scientific matters, even these beginnings were desultory, and the source of the general run of twentieth-century criticism is to be found in a period as recent as the nineteenth century.

It is not the intention of the present essay to attempt to fill this considerable gap by furnishing a complete critique of literary investigation;

rather, the aim is to direct attention to a central question that has been solved in music and the plastic arts, but which has been generally neglected in literature. The problem referred to is the analysis of structural forms and the manner in which such an analysis can aid in delineating the attitudes that lie behind these forms. It is an indication of the still inchoate condition of literary studies that the mention of form in literature ordinarily meets with either bewilderment or uncomprehending hostility.

In the study of the plastic arts and music, a reference to form is readily understood, for the apparatus of the investigation of structure is a common possession among all students of these arts. One of the urgent needs of literary study at present is the development of a common body of procedure and terminology in the description of forms. Although it is something of a novelty, the study of these matters in literature is not entirely unknown. In the present generation, the work of Joaquín Casalduero in Spanish literature (and in particular that concerning Cervantes' works), constitutes a model of procedure in formal analysis. Likewise, Imbrie Buffum's work on Agrippa d'Aubigné's *Les tragiques* is a solid contribution to the understanding of structure in non-dramatic poetry. The work of a number of American critics, including Cleanth Brooks and John Crowe Ransom, offers perhaps the most considerable body of contemporary effort in this direction. In the preceding generation and in a completely different field, Gilbert Murray as early as 1913 demonstrated a grasp of the formal functions of the chorus in Euripides' plays.[1] These critics, however, and the relatively small number of other scholars who have shown an awareness of form in literature are quite exceptional, and their significance is too little appreciated. The typical critic of the twentieth century is unversed in the valuable lessons that the other arts and their critical literatures are capable of teaching concerning the paramount importance of inquiry into the mode of construction in a work of art. It is for this reason that the questions of formal analysis, which are an established part of criticism in music, painting, sculpture, and architecture have been almost universally ignored in literature. The larger part of the recent investigations of literature merely plough again the already well-cultivated ground of such categories as positivistic cause and effect, the rules of 'regular' tragedy, or the relative excellence of various modes of dealing with the psychology of characters.

The frequent references to the plastic arts that will appear herein should not create the impression that the present intention is to engage in a direct comparison of the theater with those arts. Painting, sculpture, architecture, and music are mentioned only to indicate that all the arts share in a single complex of esthetic prepossessions and that their forms demonstrate it in a recognizable way. It is assumed that the arts of a given era proceed from a common attitude toward artistic creation and that this attitude finds expression in the various specific arts, including literature.

It is not the aim of this study to offer an explanation for the whole culture of the two periods involved, nor for the less considerable although still formidable question of the entire range of the literature of the time. The real objective is to come to grips with the problem of the various stages of esthetic development through which the drama passed during the sixteenth and seventeenth centuries and to describe the structural traits in which these changing attitudes toward art were embodied. There is no attempt to deal exhaustively even with this reduced range of data. The procedure has been to select a limited number of plays almost at random; these works were therefore not chosen because of their conformity with an a priori theoretical formula.

The first of the six works studied, Lazare de Baïf's *Electra*, was taken because it was one of the earliest that denoted a new trend away from the medieval drama and because it was readily available. Garnier's *Hippolyte* was included both for its own sake as a sixteenth-century work and because of the comparisons that could be made between it and *Phèdre*. *Bradamante* and Hardy's *La belle égyptienne* were selected because it was considered desirable to study the tragi-comedy as well as the tragedy. The inclusion of *Le Cid* and *Phèdre* was determined by the fact that they are of such overriding importance in the seventeenth century that they could hardly be omitted.[2]

B

The necessity for an exhaustive examination of each play precluded the possibility of using any considerable number of them. This in turn called for the employment of a technique of sympathetic understanding of each work in its proper cultural and esthetic atmosphere, and at the same time made impossible any kind of statistical inquiry in regard to the categories investigated. The intention, then, has been to analyze merely a sampling of the many plays that were printed during the six-teenth and seventeenth centuries. Only now and then during the in-vestigation of these works has it been deemed advisable to attempt to arrive at a value judgment concerning them, and in every case an attempt is made to base such an opinion on the forms themselves. The tacit understanding of more than a little of latter-day criticism runs to the effect that the principal business of the critic is to make value judg-ments and to arrange works in a hierarchy of good, bad, and indifferent. In contrast, this monograph rests on the presumption that the first pre-occupation of the critic is to understand the work of art in its own immanent terms. The value judgment, when it becomes advisable or necessary, will follow naturally and easily upon the process of compre-hension, as will its ranking on a scale of excellence. The appreciation and enjoyment of a work of art, like its ranking on a scale of excellence, are not to be despised and indeed are much to be sought for, but these desirable experiences must follow understanding rather than precede it.

Among the large majority of those who are working in literature, there exists the tenacious conviction that the sixteenth-century French theater is nothing more than a period of preparation for something better that made its appearance in the seventeenth century. Back of this belief lies the unexpressed feeling that art, like material technology and biological science, is susceptible of explanation in terms of progress from lower to higher forms. This point of view is unequivocally rejected in the investigation now in hand, and in its place is substituted the conviction that each period of art history evolves its own peculiar ideal of beauty which is neither better nor worse than the ideals of other epochs. This assumption enables the critic to dispense with the quasi-moral attitudes of approval and condemnation and to arrive with greater facility at the attainment of the goal of understanding. It is assumed as a necessary condition of this understanding that the investigator must perceive that each period of literary history, like those of music, painting, architecture, and sculpture, creates its own distinctive pattern of artistic forms peculiar to itself and not reproduced elsewhere in its entirety. The comprehension of these characteristic forms leads directly to a grasp of the creative process by means of which the writer produced a work of literary art. It is for this reason that the investigation of structure is of first importance as a critical method.

It can be stated further, as one of the underlying tenets of this study, that differences in formal patterns serve to define the separate periods in the drama, just as is the case with the plastic arts and music. Thus, the sixteenth century has a distinctive way of handling plot, character, and linguistic style that is characteristically different, as a total pattern, from the corresponding forms of any other period of art history. One must keep carefully in mind that it is the total pattern which is distinctive. Single traits that are similar may occur in other periods, although even in these cases similarity is not identity. It follows, therefore, that it is possible to define an era in the history of the theater in terms of its peculiar modes of creating plots, characters, and style, that is, in terms of its salient, characteristic modes of construction. The effort herein will be to perform this service for the French drama of the sixteenth and seventeenth centuries. The method will be to define their respective epochal attitudes toward art by analyzing specific dramatic works. It must be understood that the individual artist's esthetic, while not determined by this epochal spirit in a mechanical cause and effect manner, is largely conditioned by it, at the same time that his practices help to determine those of his period. Art depends on a complex of traditional attitudes toward artistic expression and on the conventional apparatus by means of which it is incorporated in concrete works; these are furnished by the culture in which the artist lives. At the same time, it must be understood that art is not produced by formula. The individual is capable of introducing innovations and is able to run the scale of a

limited number of variations on this cultural ideal, but he is incapable
of discarding it *in toto* and creating a wholly new art.

For the purposes of the present work, structural forms in literature
may be defined as the configurations that the various parts assume when
they are put together to create a unified whole. More specifically, form
in the theater is the characteristic way in which the plot, the personages,
and the language are organized in order to create the work of art. The
importance of formal studies in criticism can hardly be exaggerated.
The object of the critic is always to understand a work of art in its own
peculiar and specific terms; the comprehension of the structure of an
art work leads directly to this desired understanding, at least in part.
The study of formal organization is consequently a pressing necessity
because it contributes directly to the attainment of the only goal proper
to criticism. In analyzing form in the drama, therefore, it has been
found indispensable to examine the three elements of plot, characters,
and linguistic style. The analyses that are included herein will investi-
gate these factors in considerable detail, as well as other less fundamental
matters which vary from one play to another. The basic similarities of
the Renaissance and the Baroque will be largely ignored, on the ground
that differences are more significant than resemblances in the study and
definition of two successive periods of art history. To refer frequently
to the similarities of two epochs is to leave the impression that they constitute one period rather than two. If the plastic arts of the Renaissance
and those of the Baroque be lumped together and contrasted with the
art of the twentieth century, it will be apparent that the art of these
earlier periods is representational, while that of the twentieth century
is non-representational in nature. Such a classification implies similarity
and ignores the essential cleavage between the arts of the sixteenth and
seventeenth centuries; it is precisely the distinctions between them that
constitute the critical point in the understanding of the attitudes of these
epochs toward art.

A possible objection concerning the use of various plays inspired by
Greek or Latin originals must be considered. It has been often assumed
that a translation or adaptation is not an original work and hence cannot

represent any indigenous concept of art. This objection may be answered as follows: If it is desired to push the analysis of the theater back to the earliest possible manifestations of the Renaissance spirit (i.e. to the early sixteenth century), it becomes necessary to study the translations, since nothing else is available. Moreover, a translation will give some indication of the nature of the artistic will of the time, for even a close rendition must undergo a transformation of some sort that will inevitably reflect the newly emerging esthetic attitudes. It is impossible to draw a line of demarcation between close translation on the one hand and free adaptation on the other during the sixteenth century in France. Even in a version that attempts to follow the original closely, the style perforce cannot constitute a mere duplication of the older version in the new language, and consequently there can be nothing in the nature of a close imitation of the form and spirit of the language of the original.[3] This linguistic discrepancy constitutes an irreducible minimum of difference which guarantees that a translation cannot be a mere re-expression of the primitive version in another medium. It must also be kept in mind that even if plot and characters follow the older work faithfully, this occurs because it contains elements that appeal to the adapter in one or more of its traits. Presumably, a sixteenth-century translation, even a relatively faithful one, embodies to some extent the artistic strivings of the current period rather than those of a previous era. Hence, it has been deemed expedient in the problem now in hand to assume that any play in French represents an expression of the prevailing concept of art in the drama. The present analyses, therefore, will not refer to the originals of any of the works that are studied, since they are considered to be irrelevant insofar as the present purpose is concerned.

A point of theory regarding a matter of general procedure demands careful explanation. In dealing with any body of phenomena, it is essential to start with a preconceived working hypothesis. Obviously, such a body of theory is of heuristic value only if the investigator is both willing and determined to engage in a constant revision of the hypothesis in order to bring it in line with new facts elicited during the investigation. In the course of the inquiry that follows, the assumptions were

reviewed and revised as each play was analyzed. As a result, some portions of the theory had to be discarded in their entirety. This signifies
that the definitions of Renaissance and Baroque in the French theater
are generalized and abstract in nature. It cannot be assumed that all of
the definitions will apply to any single play, nor will any one work
serve to illustrate all of the principles laid down. The definitions as
given are designed to describe the period as a whole and can be applied
to each play only in general terms. The specific application of these
abstractions to particular works will be found in the several analyses.

A word concerning terminology is in order. The term 'Renaissance'
is used to refer to a vaguely defined chronological period of art history
that begins about 1500 and shades into a new era toward the end of the
century. 'Sixteenth century' is synonymous with 'Renaissance,' except
in those cases where the context makes a different meaning obvious. In
the same way, 'seventeenth century' and 'Baroque' are used as
approximate equivalents.[4]

A reproach has been entered against the word 'Baroque' to the effect
that it is meaningless, or that it has a significance so broad and so fluid
that it is useless as a term of art history. This criticism, which is without
foundation where music and the plastic arts are concerned, has a certain validity in literary studies, but only because the study of form in
literature is still in its nascent stages. It is the purpose of this monograph to attempt to furnish a precise definition of Baroque as well as
Renaissance in the single narrow area of the French theater during these
periods. The application of these definitions to other plays than the six
considered here and to other literary genres furnishes material for future
labor.

Notes

1 Gilbert Murray, *Euripides and His Age* (New York, 1913), pp. 226–43. See especially pp. 232–41.

2 It was originally planned to include in this study these plays: Jodelle, *Didon se sacrifiant* (1558); Hardy, *Didon se sacrifiant* (*c.* 1593–1600); and Quinault, *Les coups de l'amour et de la fortune* (1657). All three works were analyzed in detail but it was found that the trajectory of formal changes could be outlined satisfactorily with only six plays rather than with the nine that were examined. Hence, the three works mentioned were omitted for the sake of brevity.

3 Baïf's *Electra* furnishes an illustrative instance of this principle, as Sturel's remarks indicate. 'Mais les traductions trop brèves sont rares chez Baïf: son défaut serait plutôt d'allonger le texte . . . il ne faut pas prendre au pied de la lettre la déclaration de Baïf sur le titre de l'édition de 1537, *Traduicte ligne pour ligne et vers pour vers.*' (René Sturel, 'Essai sur les traducteurs du théâtre grec en français avant 1550', *Revue d'histoire littéraire de la France*, xx [1913], p. 278.)

4 It may be apropos to point out that the numbers '1500–1700' in the title of the present volume are simply a kind of shorthand for 'sixteenth and seventeenth centuries.'

1

Definition of Renaissance and Baroque in the French Theater

Since the publication of a previous volume concerning the application of Wölfflin's theories to the Spanish theater, it has become apparent that the statements which served to adapt his five principles to the analysis of dramatic plot were unsatisfactory. It was evident, first, that a full consideration of the forms of the drama demanded that these statements be expanded so as to include the characters and the linguistic style. It also became clear that the formal descriptions of the earlier book suffered from an excessively close dependence on categories that had been created for the plastic arts. Hence, it was necessary to develop a descriptive framework that would apply specifically to the theater, although without dispensing with the considerable benefits still to be had from Wölfflin's work. The enlarged concepts that are offered here were drawn from three sources—some suggestions that have been retained from Wölfflin's *Principles of Art History*, experience in the analysis of several additional Spanish plays of the sixteenth and seventeenth centuries, and a careful revision of the resulting tentative principles during the course of the examination of the French works that are included in the present investigation. On this basis, the forms of the French drama of the Renaissance and Baroque periods may be described in the following terms:

RENAISSANCE

Plot. There is only one plot and therefore the idea of the fusion of the chief motive with the subplots does not arise. Within the framework of a single, obviously dominant plot, each scene is clearly distinct from all the others but is subordinated to the principal theme. As in the plastic arts of the Renaissance, the work of art is made up of separate and well-defined parts whose interrelationships are always clear.

In the drama, time is conceived as a number of scenes that are organized in succession along a single line of plot and which proceed steadily to the clearly anticipated ending. The time that elapses during the play is reduced to a minimum by assuming the preliminary events and concentrating on the moment of crisis in the action.

Logical development is deliberately sought. Every incident contributes with an obvious directness to the main and only plot. There is no displacement of the axis; that is, nothing detracts from the central motive.

Style. The style is uniformly elevated in tone, is lacking in humor, and makes use of figures of speech that are restrained and direct and are generally lacking in ornamentation and bizarre relationships. The emotional tone is impersonal and restrained, and is characterized by a slow and steady rise in tension until the last scene or two. Such distracting elements as humor and seemingly irrelevant soliloquies are absent. Speeches are often characterized by a highly formal organization along obviously logical lines. The general mood of the language is one of an unvaryingly elevated tone and an even, majestic dignity. All these qualities contribute to the feeling of clarity and inevitability in the plot.

Characters. The characters are uniformly majestic and serious. Their personalities and interrelationships remain stable and unchanging. The secondary personages function only to point at the principal character or characters, a function that is performed from the beginning of the play to the end without deviation. All relationships seem to be established and maintained according to a rigidly logical plan.

There is a paucity of cross relationships between the characters, who tend to be related in an opposed pair in the case of the protagonists. Each of the principals has a train of minor figures that are related to him or her alone in a relation of lesser to greater. All the secondary characters have this relation to one and only one of the leading actors. No relationships are allowed to develop between two or more minor actors. Because of these rigid, exclusive relations, the major personages tend to seem impersonally detached from each other, while the subsidiary figures exist only as their appendages. At the same time, they are held together by their participation in the unique plot.

BAROQUE

Plot. The plots fuse and are interwoven; they are not sharply marked off from each other. Plots and subplots are integrated and indivisible. The relations of the plots and subplots are characterized by restless and continuous movement, contrast, and a liking for the paradoxical and the bizarre. The several separate plots steadily merge with each other as if they were aiming at one principal goal. These plots finally converge at the end of the play on the chief motive. This convergence is expressed in a surprise ending concentrated in the last scene or two.

An obviously logical development of plot is avoided. The principal theme is partly obscured until the last few scenes by a number of subplots that are not strictly necessary for the development of this principal theme; but at the end, the leading motive dominates strongly. Seemingly distracting elements are introduced—e.g., subplots, descriptions, apparently irrelevant soliloquies, etc. (These correspond to the profuse Baroque decoration in the plastic arts.)

Style. The style is extravagant and makes use of contrast, humor, and figures of speech that involve far-fetched conceits. The emotional tone is soft, intimate, and extravagant, and is characterized by a deliberately fluctuating tension. There is a fondness for the paradoxical and the bizarre.

The figure of speech tends to have such ornamentation as a marked deviation from the normal syntactic order, puns, and an obvious parallelism of grammatical form that encloses contradictory ideas.

Characters. All of the characters are capable of both seriousness and humor. Their personalities and the relationships between them are unstable and often ambiguous. There is a fondness for the paradoxical and the bizarre in these relations. The secondary personages function only to focus attention on the leading character or characters, but this process reaches its culmination in the last scene or two and becomes fully apparent only then. There is a pronounced displacement of the axis; that is, the central characters are kept from seeming the most important until at or near the end.

2

Lazare de Baïf, *Electra* (1537) [1]

SUMMARY OF PLOT AND PLOT SCHEME

Scene i (pp. A4 recto–A5 verso)—Orestes and his tutor outline briefly the antecedents of the play. Orestes reveals that he has come to kill Clytemnestra and Aegisthus. They hear Electra approaching and leave.

Scene ii (pp. A5 verso–B4 verso)—Electra reviews the past events and the present situation of her misery. The chorus sympathizes with her.

Scene iii (pp. B4 verso–C1 verso)—Chrysosthemis enters on the way to place gifts from Clytemnestra at Agamemnon's grave. She tells Electra of a mysterious dream that Clytemnestra has had that seems to foretell that Agamemnon will be avenged. In compliance with Electra's request, Chrysosthemis promises not to place the gifts at Agamemnon's tomb.

Scene iv (pp. C1 verso–C5 recto)—Clytemnestra and Electra denounce each other. Their bone of contention is Agamemnon's death and the events preceding and following it.

Scene v (pp. C5 recto–C8 verso)—The Tutor enters and tells Clytemnestra and Electra that Orestes is dead. He recounts the manner of his supposed demise at some length. Clytemnestra rejoices and Electra expresses her despair. Clytemnestra takes the Tutor into the palace.

Scene vi (pp. C8 verso–D2 verso)—Electra laments her misfortune as the chorus extends its sympathy.

Scene vii (pp. D2 verso–D7 recto)—Chrysosthemis comes from Agamemnon's grave and reports that someone has poured out libations on it. This signifies that Orestes is alive and has come to take revenge on Clytemnestra. Electra tells her that Orestes is dead. She asks Chrysosthemis to kill Aegisthus but Chrysosthemis refuses.

Scene viii (pp. D7 recto–D8 recto)—The chorus speaks of Electra's unhappy situation.

Scene ix (pp. D8 recto–E6 verso)—Orestes reveals his identity, and Electra and the chorus rejoice.

Scene x (pp. E6 verso–E8 recto)—The Tutor tells them that everything is going according to plan. He and Orestes leave to seek out Clytemnestra and kill her.

Scene xi (pp. E8 recto–F1 verso)—Electra and the chorus discuss her imminent revenge. Orestes kills Clytemnestra off-stage.

Scene xii (pp. F2 recto–F2 verso)—Orestes enters and tells Electra that Clytemnestra is dead. He hides and Aegisthus enters.

Scene xiii (pp. F2 verso–F4 verso)—Aegisthus gloats over Orestes' death, of which he has heard. Orestes enters, seizes him, and takes him away to kill him.

Plot. An examination of the summary of the plot indicates that the theme of revenge for Agamemnon's murder is dominant throughout the play. No other motive exists and therefore the concept of the interweaving of plot and subplots has no occasion to arise. Within the framework of this unique theme, each scene stands relatively separate from its immediate neighbors in time. This Renaissance habit of thinking of scenes as discrete divisions of the plot-material is apparent, for example, in the manner of moving from scene iv to scene v. In iv, Clytemnestra and Electra engage in a furious mutual denunciation. Electra accuses her mother of murder and fornication, and is answered with counter-accusations of willful ingratitude and foolishness. Scene v opens when Clytemnestra calls for the necessary materials for an oblation before her prayer to Phoebus. The strong feelings of the angry charges and countercharges of the preceding division do not carry over into the new scene. Clytemnestra's attitude changes abruptly and completely from one of fury against Electra and Agamemnon to one of fear that the dream she has had presages some disaster that is about to overtake her. The first few lines of scene v read as follows (p. C4 verso):

Ça les oblations, apporte moy mamye
Pleines de tous bons fruictz, affin que dieu ie prie
Qu'il luy plaise m'oster la frayeur que iay eue
De male vision, qu'en mon dormant ay veue.
O Phébus protecteur de chacune maison
Ie te supplie entendz ma secrette oraison . . .

In the transition from one scene to the next, Clytemnestra's nature
does not change but her emotional attitude undergoes a radical and
sudden transformation. This feeling of separateness between the divisions of the play is reinforced by the settled custom of ending each
scene with a speech or phrase that has the sound of finality and
functions to put an end to one part as the next begins. Scene iv is con-
cluded by two lines spoken by Electra (p. C5 recto):

Ie te laisse, et le veuil, prie tant que vouldras,
Car parolle de moy oultreplus tu ne oyras.

Scene x ends when Orestes and the Tutor leave to seek out Clytemnestra. Orestes puts a definite period to this scene by saying (p. E8 recto):

Pylade, nostre faict plus ne veult long propos,
Ains nous y fault aller à ce paire dispos,
Après que nous aurons aux ymaiges des dieux
Fait honneur et salut, qui habitent ces lieux.

In order to provide an effective conclusion for scene vii, Chrysosthemis says (p. D7 recto):

Ie m'en vaiz, car ie veoy qu'en vain parle et labeure:
Mon propos ne peult estre à toy bien gracieux,
Et ie ne puys louer ton cueur audacieux.

The end of the play is signified by a few concluding lines that fall
into this same pattern. The chorus says (p. F4 verso):

O genre d'Atréus, après qu'a bien souffert
Tu as ta liberté à peine recouuert,
Par hardement
Finablement.

Not every scene of the play has the usual formal ending, but, even when it is missing, the feeling of a definite transition from one discrete part to another is still given by the abrupt and complete change in the topic under discussion. The change from scene iii to iv is bridged by the chorus. The last few lines of iii and the first few lines of iv read as follows (p. CI verso):

Chorus
Car depuys que fut submergé
Myrtilus, et de coups chargé,
Et vilainement mys à mort,
Mercure courroucé du tort
A tousiours enuoyé malheur
En la maison, et chassé l'heur.

Clytemnestra
Ie to veoy derechef dehors estre, à ta guise:
Egistus est absent, qui tenoit ta franchise
Deffendant de sortir . . .

All this points to a characteristic Renaissance procedure. It is never the function of any single scene to direct attention onward to the future action of the play, for each part is relatively self-contained. In accordance with the artistic prepossessions of the time, the several scenes of the *Electra* are arranged in succession along the single line of plot. Each scene is distinctly different in its subject matter from those that immediately precede and follow, while at the same time all of them are integrated by their close relation to the unique motif. This detachment of parts involves a mode of handling plot that is analogous to the separation of the figures from each other in a Renaissance painting. Just as in the picture, each object is carefully set apart from the adjoining forms.

In much the same way, the scenes of the present play are detached from each other.

This relationship can be understood better if it is placed in contrast with the procedure adopted by the dramatists of the Baroque. Under the guidance of these concepts, the authors of this later epoch organized plot on the radically different basis of a highly complex interweaving of several parts. Each of these parts was related to all the others in such a way that the minor themes united with the major at the end of the play and gave the effect of a convergence of all the themes toward an ideological and formal point. In the Renaissance theater, the author created a series of carefully separated scenes, characterized by unequivocal relationships, all tending to induce a steady, well-marked progress to the clearly anticipated ending. In the Baroque, the approach to the denouement proceeds by means of scenes that are tangled together in apparent disorder, with fluid, uneasy relations whose effect is to conceal partly the carefully prepared conclusion.

For the Renaissance artist, the point does not reside in presenting the action of the story, for that is regarded as given and fully known from the beginning. Interest lies in presenting in dignified, sonorous language a series of static tableaux whose content can cause no surprise to the audience.[2] In the *Electra*, Baïf followed the standard Renaissance practice of assuming that the spectators were sufficiently familiar with the story to need no introduction to it. This enabled him to dispense with all the preliminaries and get on with the business in hand. It is this difference from the practice of the Baroque that explains the general tendency during the sixteenth century to restrict its subjects to those of Greek and Roman literature. It is not that they attempted to copy the esthetic ideals of these earlier periods, but rather that they chose them because their potential audiences were thoroughly acquainted with them.

Time is thought of as a number of units that are arranged in a strict sequence along a single line of plot. Each scene deals with its assigned subject, and the following division then turns to a different topic that still has an obvious connection with the story of revenge. This arrangement

2. Vermeer: Officer and Laughing Girl

1. Raphael: Madonna in the Meadows

4. Interior of the Church of Wies, Upper Bavaria

3. Rubens: Martyrdom of Saint Liévin

is analogous to a number of beads strung on a wire; each scene is separate from the contiguous parts, while all of them are held firmly together by the sole theme. The natural issue of the progression of these isolated blocks of time is the inevitable denouement, which is made apparent from the first scene.

All this implies a peculiar mode of attaining unity in the sixteenth century which is as evident in the theater as in the other arts. In the plastic arts of the Renaissance, unity is attained through a number of seemingly separate and relatively independent parts that are held together by an overriding motive. The unity of plot that is achieved in *Electra* follows this same pattern; that is, the scenes give the effect of being detached from each other but at the same time they all have an unmistakable connection with the single plot of Orestes' and Electra's vengeance on Clytemnestra. The perennial dominance of the one theme is apparent in scene x, where Orestes repeatedly mentions the necessity for haste in dispatching Clytemnestra. He says to Electra (p. E6 recto):

> Laisse le superflu, mieulx vault que l'on se taise . . .
>
> .   .   .   .
>
> Car le parler perdroit nostre opportunité.
>
> .   .   .   .
>
> Car quand à plain souhait bien fortunez serons
> Alors en liberté nous nous resiouyrons.

Later he refers again to the urgency of their business (p. E8 recto):

> Pylade, nostre faict plus ne veult long propos,
> Ains nous y fault aller à ce faire dispos,
> Après que nous aurons aux ymaiges des dieux
> Fait honneur et salut, qui habitent ces lieux.

Although it is apparent by this time that Clytemnestra will be killed, the author still takes care to keep attention focused on this capital event. These admonitions act as a running obbligato that is designed to remind the audience of the nature of the denouement. This dominance of the

c

single plot is so pervasive that it persists even under circumstances that
are distinctly favorable to a feeling of mystery in the plot. In scene
ii, Electra refers to Orestes' return as highly problematical (p. A8 verso):

> Son retour me semble estre vng songe,
> Il dit tousiours qu'il veult venir
> Mais le chemin n'en peult tenir.

Tension could conceivably be allowed to arise in this situation over
Electra's uncertainty. It will often happen in the Baroque drama that
doubt will be deliberately created, not merely in the mind of one of
the characters but also in that of the audience, so that the course of the
story will be in question for some time. The Renaissance artist, however, thinks in other terms. The atmosphere of inevitability is so over-
powering and the interest so concentrated on the clearly perceived
denouement that tension over Electra's uncertainty cannot arise.

As a further contrast between these two different conceptions of art,
it may be remarked that the usual Baroque play prefers to use the
technique of interweaving a number of plots in a highly complex
manner; a secondary motive often opens the play but is dropped after
a scene or two and another line of action is taken up. After a suitable
interval, the first plot enters again but is once more set aside for a third.
The outcome of this technique is an ending that is concealed until the
last few scenes of the play and is then revealed with startling effect. The
diametrical opposition of Renaissance ideals with those of the Baroque
is demonstrated in this respect, as in others that will be considered.

The time that elapses during the play is reduced to a minimum. After
the single line of action begins, it is not interrupted; in the present case,
it obviously covers only the amount of time that is required to present
it on the stage. This is made possible by the assumption that the audience
is already well-informed concerning the play and its background, which
allows the author to proceed at once to the nub of the story without
spending time on preliminary explanations. It must be admitted that
there are frequent references in the dialog to a number of preceding

events that serve to illuminate the story of Orestes, Electra, and Clytemnestra. These explanations, however, go only as far as a casual mention of some of the salient features of the larger story and do not afford
sufficient information to provide a coherent and complete background
for the present events. It is therefore evident that the author assumes a
previous knowledge of the pertinent Greek legends and that he does
not intend to attempt their full elucidation. It will be seen that this
dense concentration of time is, in general, peculiar to the Renaissance
and that it does not regularly carry over into the Baroque drama.

One of the notable characteristics of the sixteenth-century drama was
the conviction that the plot must evolve through its various stages in a
logical manner, a trait that is implied in much of what has already been
said. Without entering upon the doubtful question of how far this procedure was a conscious one, it is possible to say that every incident and
every speech is made to contribute with an obvious directness to the
only plot. There is a complete absence of the tension of mystery in
scene i. As has already been indicated, the opening speech by the Tutor
points at once toward the leading theme of revenge. Orestes' first speech
is equally unequivocal. He says (p. A4 verso):

> Au temps que m'en allay au lieu diuinateur
> Qui Pythique est nommé, et n'est trouué menteur,
> Pour sçavoir le moyen de la vengeance prendre
> Des meurtriers de mon père, et le change leur rendre.
> Phébus me respondit ce que soudain orras.
> Sans targe et sans armet, entreprise feras.
> Par finesse et par dol te conuient peruenir
> A tuer les meurtriers, et deulx à chef venir.
> Puys doncq qu'auons ouy tel oracle et response,
> Va dedans ces maisons, s'ainsi te semble bonce,
> Pour en sçavoir le train, et tout nous rapporter.
> Par ce moyen pourrons au faict mieulx nous porter.

In this speech, the audience is informed that Clytemnestra and
Aegisthus will be killed by trickery rather than by an assault in force

and that it will be done without delay. In scene iii, the assurance is offered that the action is still proceeding toward the denouement that has been suggested. The chorus says (p. B8 verso):

Si ie n'ay le sens estourdy,
Diuinateur, et alourdy,
Priué de bonne opinion
En ma pronostication
Iustice bientost s'en viendra
Et en ses mains force tiendra
Et punira les malfaicteurs
Qui du meurtre furent aucteurs.

In scene vii, one of the functions of a speech by Chrysosthemis is to recall Orestes' presence and his imminent revenge on Clytemnestra and Aegisthus. She says (p. D3 recto):

Et puys après que l'euz bien cerché en tous lieux,
Ie m'approuche plus près du tumbeau doloreux,
Et auprès de la pyre ay veu d'un ieune poil
Nouuellement couppé, et là mis au soleil.
Soudain me vint au cueur que c'étoit là l'indice
Du retour d'Oreste, qui tant nous est propice . . .

In scene x, although it is by now apparent that Clytemnestra will be killed, Orestes states it again (p. E8 recto):

Pylade, nostre faict plus ne veult long propos,
Ains nous y fault aller à ce faire dispos . . .

Remarks of this kind are not to be regarded as being idle and useless, for they serve to help organize the story into its parts. In the present case, Orestes' speech puts a definite end to scene x and separates it from the scene that follows. Lines of this nature indicate that the Renaissance playwright conceives an effective direction of his plot-material in terms of a rigid, obvious form rather than in terms of an inchoate mass of

material over which there seems to be no control at all, as in the
Baroque. In order to avoid even the appearance of equating this logical
procedure of the Renaissance dramatist with the realism of the nineteenth century, it is expedient to call attention to a procedure that is far
removed from the techniques of the nineteenth century. In scene xi,
Orestes attacks Clytemnestra within the palace. Her speeches between
the beginnings of the assault and her death are as follows (pp. FI recto
and verso):

> Hé, hé, hé, hé. Las! la maison
> De secours déserté, et d'amys,
> Pleine de mortelz ennemys.
>
> . . . .
> Hélas de moy souffreteuse. Egistus, où es-tu?
>
> . . . .
> O filz, filz, ne veulx-tu
> Auoir pitié de celle
> Qui t'a conceu en elle?
>
> . . . .
> Hélas, naurée suys.
>
> . . . . . .
> Hélas, et derechef?

The nineteenth-century realist would be critical of all these speeches
on the ground that a real-life situation of this kind would never elicit
five speeches of such coherence, and in this he would be correct. Since
the sixteenth-century writer did not intend to attempt to reproduce
external reality, however, he was not bound by these considerations.
These speeches are a function of the Renaissance striving for an obvious
formal framework; they represent an effort to recount the action in
such a way as to facilitate the logical development of the plot. Here, as
well as in all other circumstances, the principles of nineteenth-century
realism are incapable of being applied to the art of the sixteenth century.

The evidence that has been given points to the Renaissance wish to
attain at every point the same absolute clarity that characterized the

plastic arts of the time. The plot is stripped to the bone by excluding every element that does not contribute to the single theme in a direct and obvious manner. The single plot is dominant at every moment. No distractions are allowed and the feeling of inevitability is carefully maintained. In obedience to a pervasive esthetic ideal, Baïf establishes an atmosphere of absolute clarity from the beginning of his work. Right up to the end of the play, the author still insists on providing guide posts to indicate that the given line of action is still being followed, even when there is no longer any apparent need for them. In scene xi, Electra says (p. E8 verso):

> De perpétrer le cas vng chascun d'eulx s'auance.
> O femmes, que plus i'ayme, attendez en silence.

The following speeches by Clytemnestra and Orestes recount step by step the action that takes place off-stage as Clytemnestra is killed. Even this is not considered sufficient. The omnipresent desire for clarity demands that Orestes shall state in so many words that she is dead. He says (p. F2 recto):

> Tout va très bien pour nous, touchant ceulx de dedans,
> Si d'Apollo l'oracle est seur et véritable:
> Car ià trespassée est la pour misérable:
> Ne crains plus que honte ayt maternelle pouuoir
> De te deshonnorer.

The determination to attain a maximum clearness is apparent.

Style. The style of the language throughout the play is elevated in tone, a quality that is sufficiently apparent to need no discussion; all levity is studiously excluded. In regard to the figures of speech, it is a notable characteristic of the *Electra* that they occur infrequently and that the author prefers to limit himself to a style that is largely narrative and dramatic. A salient instance of this practice is afforded by the Tutor's recital of Orestes' supposed death (pp. C5 verso–C7 verso); in this long recital, there is not a single trope. In those cases where figures of speech do appear, they are typical of the Renaissance mode of thinking in these matters. That is, they fall into the same rational, easily grasped patterns that distinguish plot and characters with easily perceived formal divisions and familiar comparisons. In scene i, Orestes compares his old tutor to a faithful horse (p. A4 verso):

> Des miens le plus aymé, grands signes de ce lieu
> Me monstres du vouloir qu'as tousiours vers moy eu;
> Car (comme vng bon cheval) non obstant qu'il soit vieil,
> Es perilz ne perd point le cueur, ains lieue au ciel
> L'oreille droict sans cesse, ainsi toy nous induitz
> A faire le debuoir . . .

The trope here refers to a familiar reality that involves no element of surprise and is stated in the direct, unornamented fashion of the time. It falls into the conventional formal pattern that states the comparison in two parts; this division into two elements is signaled by the presence of the words 'comme . . . ainsi . . .' which serve to establish the obvious scaffolding that the Renaissance dramatist finds agreeable to his feeling where style is concerned.

In scene viii, the chorus descants on Electra's unhappy situation. They say (p. D7 recto):

> Nous qui voyons la prouidence
> Des oyseaulz, et leur grand prudence,
> Lesquels esmeuz d'une pitié
> Naturelle, et grand amytié,
> Donnent aux aultres nourriture
> Desquelz sont sortis, et ont cure
> De leur rendre le bien pour le bien.
> Nous pourtant, nous n'en faisons rien,
> Mais par la fouldre et la tempeste
> Du grand dieu, et le droit céleste
> Longtemps impuniz ne seront
> Ceulx qui en mal se trouueront.

The comparison between the natural kindness of birds to their kind and man's cruelty to his is conventional and easy to comprehend. It has the usual, obvious division into two parts, the first of which begins 'Nous qui voyons,' while the second opens with 'Nous pourtant.' The predilection for a readily perceptible formal organization is as apparent here as elsewhere in the style. Again in the same scene, the chorus refers to Electra's sorrow over Agamemnon's death in these terms:

> Electra seulle est tempestée,
>
> .   .   .   .
>
> Prenant passetemps à son deul,
> Ainsi que fait le roussigneul . . .

The conventional character of the trope and the clear structural organization provided by the 'ainsi' are indications of the Renaissance wish to avoid surprises in the style as well as in the plot. In scene i, Orestes uses the same kind of easily understood simile (p. A5 verso):

> . . . ie prendz en aduantaige
> D'apparoistre soudain, comme vng astre ou oraige
> A mes faulz ennemys . . .

Equally typical of the dialog is the organization of ideas along obviously logical lines, which puts in an appearance whenever there is a difference of opinion between two characters. In discussing Electra's recalcitrance, Chrysosthemis approaches it as though it were a problem to be solved by weighing carefully all the factors on either side of the question. She says (scene iii, pp. B4 verso–B5 recto):

> Pour quoy faiz derechief, o seur, diz moy de grâce,
> Tes plainctes et douleurs icy en la court basse?
> Et par longueur de temps nullement veulx apprendre
> Nous faire aulcun plaisir, ny subicte tey rendre.
> Ie sçay bien et congnoys (quant est à mon endroit)
> Que mon cueur est dolent, et venger se vouldroit
> Des choses qu'auons veu, et si i'auoys puissance,

> Bientost leur monstreroys ce que contre eulx ie pense,
> Mais es maulx de présent, il fault caller la voile
> Si ne voulons cuyder de prendre aux dentz l'estoille,
> Et sans leur faire mal, en vain nous tourmenter.
> De ce (seur) ie vouldroys te pouuoir contenter,
> Et si sçay bien pour vray, que le droict est pour toy
> Et pour ton iugement, mais raison est pour moy,
> Car s'il fault que viuons en libre franchise,
> Obéir fault aux grandz, et tout faire à leur guise.[3]

It is worthy of note here not only that Chrysosthemis makes a direct appeal to reason but also that the entire speech is imbued with a logical rationalism. The same observations can be made with equal force with regard to Clytemnestra's defense of her past and present activities. She admits her guilt and then proceeds to justify herself (scene iv, pp. C2 recto–C2 verso):

> Car ton père, lequel tousiours pleurs et lamentes,
> Seul entre tous les Grecz fist venir en ses tentes
> Ta seur, pour l'immoler cruellement à dieu,
> Et n'eut pas tant de mal à l'affaire que i'eu.
> Oultreplus, apprendz-moy, en faueur de qui fusse
> Qu'il la sacrifia? pour les Gregoys donc fut-ce?
> Mais à eulx n'est permys qu'ilz tuassent la mienne.
> Pour son frère l'occist, aussi qu'elle estoit sienne,
> Et à moy, quoy? mon lot en étoit-il perdu?
> Pensoit-il la tuer sans qu'il fust cher vendu?
> N'auoit Ménélaus deux enfans qui viuoyent,
> Lesquelz plustost mourir, que ma fille deboyent?
> Car ils étoyent issuz et des pères et mères
> En la faueur desquelz partirent les galères.
> Auoit enfer plus grand désir d'auoir mon fruict
> Que le sien, pour qui fut la guerre en si grand bruit?
> La père auoit-il mys hors l'amour de sa fille,
> Laquelle auoit portée honneste et tant gentille,
> Et vouloit plus de bien aux filles de son frère?

N'est-ce signe évident d'un fol et mauluais père?
Ainsi le doibz penser, ores pose que soys
D'opinion contraire: et si ta seur pouuoys
Ouyr parler d'embas, ainsi le diroit elle.
Quant à moy, ie n'ay peur qu'on m'extime cruelle
Pour la vengeance faicte, et n'en ay repentence:
Et ie qui tiens pour moy, de fait iuste sentence
Si ie te semble auoir mauluaise oppinion,
Diz le moy par doulceur sans repréhension.

The rationalistic nature of this speech finds expression not only in the
careful arrangement of the arguments but also in the presence of an
introductory word for each part—'car ... oultreplus ... ainsi ... quant
à moy ...' Words of this kind lend the support of a rigid framework
that gives these lines the easily perceived construction that the Renaissance found pleasing. The last two lines of the speech function as a
formal introduction to Electra's rebuttal. She says (pp. C2 verso–C3
verso):

Ie te dy que tu diz parolle à toy infâme,
Mon père auoir tué, toy qui estoys sa femme,
Soit à tort ou à droict, rien n'est plus deshonneste.
Oncq vng tel cas ne fist la plus cruelle beste
Qui soit en les déserts, et te diz dauantaige
Que l'as fait sans raison ...

. . . .

Iadis mon père fut (ainsi qu'entendz) chasser
Au boys de Diana, pour là son temps passer,
Et prit un cerf courable, ayant grande rameure:

. . . .

Malgré luy l'imola, pour aux Grégoys complaire:
Non pour Ménélaus, et s'il l'eust fait mourir
Pour luy (comme disoys), le voulant secourir
Le failloit-il pourtant ainsi mourir par toy?
Diz-moy par quel raison? par quel droict, par quel loy?

. . . .

Et diz-moy (s'il te plaist) or par quelle achoison
A présent choses faiz tant infâmes et ordes,
Qui auec le meurtrier de ton mary t'accordes?
. . . .
Mais te semble-il au vray, chose bien fort estrange
Si vng tel cas ne peult auoir de moy louange?
Possible que diras (pour excuse fragile)
Que tu te veulx venger de la mort de ta fille.
L'excuse n'en vault rien, car il n'est raisonnable
Pour la fille espouser l'ennemy exécrable.
Mais oultre n'en diray, car moy t'admonester
Tu ne peulx endurer, sans fort te tempester . . .

Here, just as in Clytemnestra's preceding speech, the careful arrangement of the argument and the appeal to logic are supported by the division of the speech into definitely separate parts by such words as 'Ie te
dy . . . et te diz dauantaige . . . Iadis . . . Diz-moy par quel raison . . . Et
diz-moy (s'il te plaist) . . . Mais te semble . . . Mais oultre n'en diray . . .'
The frequent occurrence of formal introductions to a following speech
operates, in the same way as those qualities that have been discussed, to
organize plot and dialog in a carefully logical way. In scene v, Clytemnestra signals to the audience that the nub of the scene is about to begin
when she says (p. C5 verso):

Faiz ton debuoir, entendz, dy-moy la vérité,
Le moyen de sa mort soit à moy récité.

In scene vii, Electra's single line serves in the same capacity of an
obvious preliminary to Chrysosthemis' disclosure that Orestes has
visited his father's tomb. Her remark, 'Si tu y prendz plaisir, diz-moy
ce qu'en as veu,' is designed to let the spectators know that a disclosure
of more than ordinary interest is to follow.

A negative observation concerning a quality that does not exist in
Electra will facilitate the understanding of the differences between the
art of the sixteenth century and that of the seventeenth. It is a settled

habit in the high Baroque to enclose mutually contradictory ideas in
closely similar structural forms, usually in successive lines or half-lines.
In a number of cases in the present play, the structural parallelism occurs
but there is a notable absence of the expression of contrastive ideas. In
scene iii, Electra and Chrysosthemis exchange a long series of alternating single lines which read, in part, as follows (p. B6 verso):

Chrysosthemis
Où sont tes espéritz? veulx-tu ainsi mourir?
Electra
Affin que loing de vous puisse prendre la fuyte.
Chrysosthemis
De ta vie aultrement n'es-tu point solicite?
Electra
Belle est pour faire feste, et s'en esmerueiller.
Chrysosthemis
Belle, si tu vouloys par moy te conseiller.
Electra
A estre ne m'apprendz des amys négligente.
Chrysosthemis
Non, non, mais qu'aux seigneurs tu soys obédiente.
Electra
Toy, toy, faiz-leur la court, ma façon n'est pas telle.
Chrysosthemis
Ne tumber par mauluais conseil, est façon belle.
Electra
Tumber ie vueil, s'il fault mon père ainsi venger.

Two distinctions between this procedure and that of the Baroque are
worthy of consideration in the present connection. The succession of
lines is so arranged that the conceptual pairs of accusation and rebuttal
into which they naturally fall are not rhymed. This suggests that Baïf
did not have the same conscious striving in these matters as did the
Baroque playwright, whose preoccupation with parallelism of form in
such cases will lead him to rhyme the lines that are placed in opposition

to each other. The rhymes under such circumstances will act to call attention to the opposition of the two lines involved. The effect of stichomythic dialog in the sixteenth-century theater is to slow down the action, while in that of the Baroque it accelerates the tempo and sharpens whatever feeling of conflict there may be in the situation. The second distinction to be made between the two periods in question is that whereas the seventeenth century consciously creates ideological contrasts in such cases, the sixteenth century is not aware that the opportunity for such oppositions exists. The sharp disagreement between Electra and her sister constitutes a highly favorable set of circumstances for the statement of opposite concepts in parallel forms, but no constructions of this nature are presented. The author conceives these pairs of lines in terms of a quasi-narrative style that moves from one idea to a complementary idea and merely leads the mind to a new concept rather than presenting another that opposes the first one. In scene viii, Electra and Chrysosthemis again engage in the exchange of parallel lines. They say in part (p. D6 verso):

> Electra
> Grief est, qu'en disant bien, mal extime m'en vient.
> Chrysosthemis
> Tu as dit droictement le vice qui te tient.
> Electra
> Ne scez-tu que mon dire est de droicte iuste et fort?
> Chrysosthemis
> Mais quelquefoys le droict fait dommage et grand tort.

In this instance, the paired lines rhyme but the case already cited indicates that to Baïf this was an indifferent matter. The point to be made here is that the lines signally fail to fall into the pattern of opposed pairs of concepts that will be such a popular technical recourse in the following era of art history. In scene ix, there is a further occurrence of this kind. Orestes attempts to take the urn from Electra and tells her that the story of his death was a pretense (p. E3 recto):

Electra
Ne me oste, ie te pry, les choses que plus i'ayme.
Orestes
Point ne le permettray.
Electra
Las! malheureuse femme,
Orestes, si l'on me oste ainsi ta sépulture.
Orestes
Tu le gémis sans droict, de tel cas n'ayes plus cure.
Electra
Comment, plaingz-ie sans droict, mon frère qui est mort?
Orestes
Tu ne peulz tel propos tenir de luy sans tort.

Here, as in the cases already cited, the author fails to dispose the lines and rhymes in such a way as to emphasize sharply the opposition of ideas that actually does exist in the passage.

A further difference between the practices of the Renaissance and the Baroque appears in the use of the double-entendre. This device, which is rare in the sixteenth century, occurs in the dialog between Electra and Aegisthus soon after Clytemnestra's death. Aegisthus, who has heard of Orestes' death, comes in looking for more good news (scene xiii, pp. F2 verso–F3 recto):

Egistus
Où sont les estrangiers? ne le veulx-tu point dire?
Electra
Léans, et si ont fait des choses pour non rire.
Egistus
Comment? l'ont ilz dit mort tout véritablement?
Electra
Non, mais ilz l'ont monstré, non pas dit seullement.
Egistus
Il nous est doncq présent pour le veoir sans obstacle?
Electra
Présent certes, et est vng merueilleux spectacle.

Egistus
Tu me faiz resiouyr, ce qui n'est ton usance.
Electra
Tu pourroys bien auoir trop grand resiouyssance.

The use of double meaning here in Electra's speeches is muted and little attention is called to it, in contrast with the more important role that it will come to play in the Baroque theater. It must be made clear that none of the comparisons that have been made between these two periods are to be interpreted as an attempt to establish an invidious distinction between them. Effort is directed solely toward an accurate description of the forms of the works under consideration, and in no case is it deemed to be a question of better or worse where the respective esthetics of the two epochs of art history are concerned.

The emotional atmosphere of the work presently under consideration is restrained and dignified, and is notably lacking in that quasi-hysterical feeling that often typifies the art of the seventeenth century. Electra's mourning over Orestes' supposed death is typical (scene ix, pp. D8 verso–E1 verso). She speaks to the urn which she thinks holds Orestes' ashes:

O monument de cil qui m'est le plus amé
De l'âme d'Oreste, qui cy est inhumé.
Las! que ie t'ay receu bien loing de l'espérance
Sur qui ie t'enuoyay, ie pensoys faire bien.
. . . .
Hélas moy malheureuse, où est la nourriture
Que par vng doux labeur t'ay fait, et par grand cure?
Allée est à néant, las tu ne fuz iamais
Tant de ta mère aymé, que de moy. Ores mais
Que puis-je deuenir?
. . . .
Ay mé mé!
O corps misérable,
Las! moy pitoyable

Ay mé mé!
O doulx chef fraternel, le malheureux chemin
Auquel ie t'enuoyay, est cause de ma fin.
Ie te prie, recoy-moy en cestuy vaisseau tien,
Moy qui suis vng néant, en toy qui n'es plus rien . . .

At the same time that there occur such emotionally charged words
as 'Las!' and 'Ay mé mé!' the feeling-tone is considerably muted
because of the prevalence of the long, sonorous line and the dignified
vocabulary that is used.

In addition to the careful restraint of the feeling-tone, a further distinction between the two periods under investigation is apparent in this
speech. Although Electra holds the urn of ashes in her hand and addresses
it directly, her remarks have nothing of the extreme preoccupation with
death that will grow up in Baroque art. The playwright of the seventeenth century would hardly have missed such an excellent opportunity to create a morbid atmosphere around the situation in which a
sister speaks to her brother's ashes. The only attempt in the present case
to take advantage of the circumstances is the single line, 'Ie te prie,
recoy-moy en cestuy vaisseau tien,' which is far different from the
feeling that a Baroque author would have been inclined to aim at in
such a scene. It is not intended to suggest that the Renaissance artist was
remiss in failing to exploit to the full the possibilities inherent in this
state of affairs, nor is there any implication that the Baroque writer was
guilty of any excess in so doing. The point to be made in the present
instance is that the two periods were guided by different conceptions of
the beautiful and inevitably found dissimilar solutions for specific
artistic problems.

For much the same reasons that have been adduced, Electra's joy at
seeing Orestes' tutor lacks the extreme tension that will be found in the
works of the seventeenth century. This emphasis on an elevated dignity
is given and maintained, of course, by a choice of language that is uniformly elevated and restrained. In scene x, Orestes presents the Tutor
to Electra, who has failed to recognize him. She says (p. E7 verso):

6. Rembrandt: Man with Golden Helmet

5. Palazzo della Cancelleria, Rome

8. Rembrandt: Christ at Emmaus

7. Bernini: Santa Teresa in Ecstasy

O iour sur tous aymé, o seul conseruateur
Des maisons d'Atrides, comment es-tu venu?
Mais es-tu cestuy-la, par qui fut retenu
Le salut de cestuy, et aussi bien de moy?
O les très chères mains, o cil qui euz en toy
Promptitude agréable à nous servir de pié,
Comment m'as-tu celé longtemps ton amytié?

In scene ii, Electra laments her own unhappy circumstances (p. B1 recto):

Mais le plus de mon âge passe
En désespoir, mon cueur se lasse:
Lasse ie suys, mon deul me myne,
Moy de parens pouure orphéline.
Nul veult aymer la désolée,
Et si suys comme vne aduolée
Traictée en la maison mon père,
Conte de moy on ne tient guère
Vous veoyez à l'acoustrement,
Regardez mon habillement.

Her remarks are touching but they do not have the intense feeling-tone common in the Baroque theater. The style is too terse and direct to permit the appearance of a semi-hysterical quality in the present case. The last two lines afford an instance of the naked, almost naive directness of the language that Baïf used.

The tension that grows up about the action of the play as a whole is characterized by a steady rise until the denouement in the last three scenes. There is no hint of the Baroque practice of using a fluctuating tension to lead up to a final, dazzling revelation at the end. The peculiar Renaissance technique of causing the tension to mount steadily until the conclusion is made possible by the permanent domination of the single motive. This insures that the story shall be known from the beginning and that the plot shall be pointed toward the denouement rather than being focused here and there on various preliminary moments.

D

The persistent drive toward absolute clarity that made itself felt in the development of plot is also at work in the linguistic style. In scene ii, Electra reviews the previous events in some detail and tells in full the reasons for her sorrow. She says (p. B3 recto):

> Premièrement, à moy, la mère qui m'a faicte,
> Me hait, et veult grand mal, et me vouldrait déffaicte.
> Après, en ma maison ie viz et si fréquente
> Auecques les meurtriers, et contre mon entente,
> D'eulx ie suys impérée, et fault que preigne d'eulx
> Ce que m'est besoing, soit chair, vin, pain et oeufz.

In scene i, the author wants the audience to know that a speech of major importance is coming. In order to achieve the necessary clearness, he has Orestes give a formal introduction to the body of his own speech. He says to his companions (p. A4 verso):

> Doncques à mon parler donne bonne audience,
> Et s'en endroict ie faulx, redresse l'ignorance.

The two speeches just cited suggest as well another quality of the Renaissance theater that will undergo a radical transformation during the period that follows. The Renaissance conceived of a drama as a series of speeches built around a static situation that is thoroughly known. The Renaissance play is, much more than that of the seventeenth century, an exercise in pure language. In order to enjoy Baïf's *Electra*, it is necessary to give oneself up to the charm of a dignified, majestic language.[4] The Baroque retains this dependence on language, as any literary work must, but it adds the element of a fast-moving action that is limited in its scope only by difficulties of staging and by various conventional prohibitions concerning propriety of action. The objection may be made that, in the case of the work now under consideration, the habit of recounting action rather than depicting it comes directly from the Greek original. But tradition hardly offers sufficient explanation, for Baïf would not have translated Sophocles' work unless he had seen something in it that suited his esthetic sense. It is the object of the present study to discover and describe that Renaissance esthetic which has its earliest manifestations in 'translations' such as Baïf's work.

The language also contributes its part to the maintenance of a perfect clearness because of the unvaryingly elevated tone already referred to and the absence of humor or other distracting factors. A carefully logical exposition of ideas lends its reinforcement to the clear development of the plot. In scene vii, Electra's suggestion that Chrysosthemis kill Aegisthus is fantastic. She succeeds, however, in giving it a plausible appearance, not by pointing out how easy it would be nor the ways in which it might be done, but by demonstrating how necessary it is. In this respect, her arguments are irrefutable. She says (pp. D4 verso–D5 recto):

> Or escoutte à présent, ce que délibéray.
> Tu scez que sans amys nous sommes demourées,
> Car le dieu des enfers nous en a séparées:
> Et tandis qu'entendoys que le frère viuoit,
> J'auoys aulcun espoir que bien tost il viendroit . . .
>
> . . . .
>
> Mais il est mort, parquoy ie n'ay attente au frère,
> Fors qu'à toy seul . . .
>
> . . . .
>
> D'aultre part, ne veoiez-tu quel réputation
> Donroys à toy et moy par telle occision?

Chrysosthemis' answer is as rational as Electra's request. She justifies her refusal by showing with well-arranged and reasonable arguments that such a deed is impossible. Her defense reads in part as follows (p. D5 verso):

> Ne veoix-tu que tu es femelle, non pas homme?
> Et peulx beaucoup moins que tes ennemis en somme?
> Et puyz ilz ont pour eulx fortune, et vent à gré,
> Mais de nous elle fuyt, et fait nostre malgré.
> Qui est celluy qui peult vng tel homme tuer

Sans inconuenient, et en malheur tumber?
Garde qu'en estant mal, nous gaignons maulx plus grands
S'il est sceu que ayons tins telz propos sur les rancz . . .

The two different emphases in this scene—on the one hand Electra's statement of the necessity for killing Aegisthus and on the other Chrysosthemis' certainty that it is impossible to do so—enable the author to argue with equal cogency in both cases and thereby to assist in preserving the desired atmosphere of clarity.

Characters. The relationships of the characters to the plot and to each other are stable and the attitudes which the audience is intended to take toward them are carefully defined, all of which contribute to the atmosphere of clarity desired in sixteenth-century art. Clytemnestra is regarded as a monster from the beginning to the end of the play. Her nature is defined early in the work when Orestes says (p. A5 verso):

O maison paternelle, à présent suys venu
Admonesté des dieux, ainsi qu'on a cogneu,
Pour te purger par droit, de l'oultraige et mesfaict
Qui par noz ennemys vers mon père fut fait.

The ruling assumption holds that Clytemnestra has committed a heinous crime and that to take vengeance on her is equivalent to a just retribution. The chorus lends a firm support to this opinion (p. A7 recto):

Fille Electre de male mère
La mort lamente de ton père
Sans iamais t'en ressasier
Autant auiourd'huy que feis hier.
Lequel par ta mère sans foy
Et sans raison, sans dieu, sans loy
Fut surpris par déception,
Et mys en la possession
Des mains de ceulx qui l'ont occis.

In scene ii, Electra reports how her mother conducted herself on the day of Agamemnon's murder (p. B3 verso):

> Sans craindre aulcunement d'Erinnis la vengeance,
> Le iour qu'il fut tué, fait dresser vne danse,
> Et immole brebis aux dieux conseruateurs
> Tousiours par chascun moys, affin qu'ilz soyent tuteurs
> De toute leur mesgnie, et fait dérision
> Du meurtre perpétré par telle occasion.

As in Pérez de Oliva's *La venganza de Agamenón* (1528), Clytemnestra regrets Orestes' death but does not yield up her role as the monster of the play. In scene v, the following exchange takes place between her and the Tutor (p. C7 verso):

> Clytemnestra
> O mon dieu qu'est cecy? est-ce vng heur misérable
> Ou bien vng vray malheur, lequel est prouffitable?
> Las! mon cas va très mal, s'il fault saluer ma vie
> Par les malheurs de moy, et toute ma mesgnie.
> Pédagogue
> Quel desplaisir as-tu (dame) de mon messaige?
> Clytemnestra
> Auoir porté enfans, c'est vng terrible ouuraige,
> Car l'on ne peult hayr cil qu'on a procréé,
> Bien qu'à nous faire mal se soit fort essayé.
> Pédagogue
> En vain (à ce que veoy) ie suys icy venu.
> Clytemnestra
> Non en vain, mon amy, de moy es retenu:
> Car, comme en vain pourroys? quand m'apporte indice
> Evident de la mort, à ma vie propice?

Throughout the play, Clytemnestra retains her character as the evil murderess and unnatural mother to whom no sympathy is due; like

her, Aegisthus is regarded as the epitome of selfishness, and everything
he and his mistress do contributes to this impression. In the same way, the
Tutor exemplifies the faithful old servant whose only purpose is to aid
his young master. Electra's personality is treated in a similar fashion;
her role of martyr because of her father's death is laid down at once
when she first appears. Her first words (p. A5 verso), spoken off-stage,
are, 'Hélas moy malheureuse.' A few lines below she speaks of her
sorrow at her father's death (p. A6 recto):

> Las! comment pouure lamente
> De mon père la dure mort . . .

In the following scene, Electra makes it clear that she is determined
to bring about the murder of Clytemnestra and Aegisthus through the
agency of Orestes. She pursues this objective with a rigid determination that is not turned aside even when she thinks Orestes is dead.
When she can no longer hope that he will come, she tries to persuade
Chrysosthemis to act in his stead. In scene vii, she says (p. D4 verso):

> Mais il [Orestes] est mort, parquoy ie n'ay attente au frère
> Fors qu'à toy seul, affin qu'auecques ceste peur
> De tuer le meurtrier n'ayes craincte ou frayeur,
> Le meurtrier Egistus . . .

After Chrysosthemis refuses to kill Aegisthus, Electra has no hope of
being able to avenge her father but she is not moved to retreat from
her defiant attitude. When Chrysosthemis suggests that she should com-
promise with what she regards as her duty, Electra replies, 'Or selon
telles loix iamais ie ne viuray.' Her independence and self-confident
strength are regarded as permanent attributes, which she retains under
all circumstances. Not even her great joy at seeing Orestes can destroy
her assurance that she is capable of forcing herself to do whatever she
thinks is necessary. When he admonishes her to conceal her rejoicing
from Clytemnestra, she says (p. E6 recto):

Et sçaiches qu'Egistus n'est pas en la maison,
Mais la mère, ouy bien, à laquelle achoyson
Aulcune ne donray, qu'elle appercoyue goutte
De la ioye que i'ay, de cela ne faiz doubte.

This rigid adherence of personality to a single narrow repertory of traits finds further expression in the bitter argument between Clytemnestra and Electra in scene iv. At every point, the audience is made to feel the viciousness of Clytemnestra's character and Electra's unyielding determination to exact vengeance for her father. It goes without saying that Orestes and Chrysosthemis have the same unchanging personalities. In every case, the characters are conceived as the embodiment of a certain small range of qualities beyond whose clearly defined boundaries they cannot and do not go. From this conception of character as immutably fixed proceeds the psychological generality of the Renaissance drama, with its pronounced tendency to think of its personages as 'types.' This manner of regarding personality is as well a part of the source of the static nature of the action commented on by Lanson.[5]

It is relevant to the purpose of the present investigation to point out an instance in which Baïf failed to develop the quality of contrast on which the Baroque will insist so strongly. The opposition between Electra's grim courage and Chrysosthemis' cowardice and meekness exists, but it remains implicit in the situation because it is not exploited by being insisted upon to the point where attention is forcibly drawn to it. It is precisely this insistence upon contrastive values in the later drama that will serve in part to distinguish it as an artistic movement with different ideals from those of the Renaissance.

Not only are the assigned personalities of the characters regarded as essentially unchanging throughout the course of the play, but the relationships between them as well are looked upon as stable and incapable of change. Orestes and Electra, who seem to function as a single character split into two parts, are the embodiment of inexorable vengeance. This, their overriding characteristic, exercises a permanent governance over their relations with Clytemnestra, Aegisthus, and the other figures. Clytemnestra and, in a subordinate fashion, Aegisthus constitute the evil principle of the play against whom this desire for vengeance is allowed to operate. The Tutor's only role is that of Orestes' aid. Chrysosthemis functions only as Electra's timid little sister. In all cases, the relationship is carefully defined and is thereafter maintained in its original terms. The secondary characters lend further support to the rational quality of the plot by pointing always at the leading figures. Chrysosthemis, Aegisthus, and the Tutor are used only to direct attention toward Electra, Orestes, and Clytemnestra. The role of the chorus as a support for Electra is obvious, as is its function to keep the single motive always in view. In the opening speech of the play, the Tutor is not allowed to speak as an individual in his own right but is required to direct the audience's attention at once to the principal line of action. He says (p. A4 recto):

> O filz d'Agamemnon, lequel iadis en Troye
> Estoit ducteur des Grecz, monstrant d'honneur la voye,
> A present tu peux veoir ce q'as tant désiré,
> Car vecy l'ancien Argos, tant espéré:
>
> . . . .
>
> Or sus doncq Orestes, et toy Pylade aussi,
> En brief fault consulter que deuons faire icy . . .

No speech is permitted to mention anything except the leading motive, in the midst of which are located the three chief figures, so that the secondary personages are forced to point at Electra, Orestes, and Clytemnestra without deviation throughout the entire play. This arrangement of characters is analogous to the physical arrangement of the figures in a Renaissance painting, in which all of them are disposed in a row extending across the foremost plane and with the principal figure or figures located in the mechanical center of this plane.[6] It is expedient here to remark by way of precaution that the intention is not to imply any direct connection between the two arts but to indicate what seems to be a clear case of a common esthetic principle that underlies both painting and the drama, and which works to produce effects that are similar but not identical.

The structure of the hierarchy of characters possesses some features that are peculiar to the present work. Instead of two principal figures, there are three—Electra, Orestes, and Clytemnestra. Both Electra and Orestes, however, function as the incarnation of a single set of emotions grouped around the ideal of revenge in the blood feud. They can, therefore, be considered as two individuals who act as one. Essentially, this structure of relationships falls into the pattern of the Renaissance play, although it is not the simple opposition of two figures that is found in such works as Jodelle's *Didon*. As has been said, the three minor personages—Chrysosthemis, Aegisthus, and the Tutor—are related only to the principals. No connections are permitted to grow up between any two secondary characters. Every action and every speech of these latter three are calculated to contribute to the development of the single line of action.

The relationships of the various minor characters may be described as follows: Chrysosthemis is related to both Clytemnestra and Electra, Aegisthus is tributary to Clytemnestra, and the Tutor is connected with the Orestes-Electra complex. Again the relations are not as simple as those of Jodelle's *Didon se sacrifiant*, where all the personages without exception have a connection with only one of the principals and where none is related to both sides after the manner of Chrysosthemis in the present instance. In a way that will become familiar during the course of the sixteenth century, the major figures—Clytemnestra and Electra-Orestes—collide in an opposed relationship that makes the two sides seem to be detached from each other. Each represents a diametrically opposed force—revenge versus escape from revenge. Each typifies a different ideal—duty to father (Electra-Orestes) versus unjust revenge and illicit love (Clytemnestra). All these formalized, obvious oppositions are held together by their inclusion within the bounds of the sole plot. This peculiar structure produces the unity of relatively independent parts that was assumed as a necessary condition of art during the Renaissance.

Notes

[1] The edition used is as follows: Lazare de Baïf, *Tragédie de Sophocle intitulée Electra* (Paris, 1537). Although it was published in 1537, *Electra* was translated before 1530. 'Peut-être devons-nous en conclure que la traduction manuscrite d'*Electra*, faite sans doute en France, a précédé le départ de Baïf pour l'Italie (25 juin 1529).' (Sturel, 'Essai sur les traducteurs du théâtre grec en français avant 1550,' *op. cit.*, p. 275.)

Subsequent references to *Electra* are to this edition and will be indicated by giving the number of the page or the scene as the case may be. The play is not divided into scenes, and the division into scenes is by the present writer. The original spelling has been preserved for the most part, but it has been found advisable to introduce a number of minor modifications in order to facilitate the reading of passages quoted from the text. These changes include the addition of punctuation where necessary, the modernization of the system of accent marks, the use of the cedilla, and the spelling in full of all abbreviations. With these exceptions, the text has been reproduced as it is in the original. The passages that have been quoted herein are from a microfilm copy of the edition cited, which is in the Bibliothèque Nationale in Paris under the call number 'Réserve Yb 1057.'

[2] This better enabled the playwright to attain his static ideal of oratorical speeches that constituted the drama of that period. The static nature of the forms is equally visible in the plastic arts. In Raphael's 'Madonna in the Meadows' (Fig. 1) the three human figures involved are disposed in a broad-based triangle that lends a general stability to the composition. Their attitudes are quiet and their bodies are in repose. There is no hint here of the interrupted gesture of the Baroque and nothing of the feeling that an action has been frozen in mid-career and then transferred to the canvas. This monumental calm is reinforced by the flat, peaceful landscape in the background. Every formal element contributes to an atmosphere of static quietness that is the epitome of the Renaissance inclination in these matters.

[3] There seems to be a typographical error in the fourth line of this passage. The word 'subicte' apparently should be 'subiecte.'

[4] The following comment was written in 1889, but the misapprehension that it represents still counts a number of votaries among the scholars of the present generation. 'Sous cette influence [i.e., of writing plays to be read rather than staged] les pièces [of the sixteenth century] sont ce qu'elles devaient être: des élégies à peine dialoguées. Les monologues abondent et forment des actes à eux seuls: lors même que plusieurs personnages sont ensemble sur la scène, ils font des discours plutôt qu'ils ne conversent, ils sont plutôt avocats dans un débat qu'acteurs véritables dans une action. Quelle action, d'ailleurs, que celle que la plupart de ces tragédies! Tout s'y passe dans les coulisses, et l'on ne nous donne sur la scène que de longs récits; les personnages en lutte ne s'y rencontrent pas et ne paraissent que succesivement devant nous.' (Eugène Rigal, *Alexandre Hardy et le théâtre français* [Paris, 1889], p. 88.) The description is passably accurate but the usual superfluous attitude of disapproval is in evidence.

[5] 'Car ils (les dramaturges du seizième siècle) ne savent ce que c'est que l'action dramatique. Elle n'est ni une ni multiple chez eux, elle n'est pas . . . De fait, leur pratique correspond à leur talent: ils traitent chaque sujet comme une succession de thèmes poétiques. Chaque situation, chaque état moral n'est pour eux qu'un motif, selon la nature duquel ils modifient leur rhétorique, écrivant ici un discours, là une ode, ailleurs une élégie . . .' (Gustave Lanson, *Histoire de la littérature française*, 14th ed. [Paris, 1920], p. 414.) These observations, which are supported in their entirety by the present analysis, indicate how

far a brilliant mind like that of Lanson could proceed in literary criticism even in the absence of effective categories under which to classify artistic phenomena and thereby interpret them correctly.

Hidden behind the contemptuous tone of Lanson's remarks is the tacit and perhaps unconscious assumption that there is a universal esthetic with which a work must conform if it is to find a place in the accepted canon of excellence. The apotheosized standard of taste here, as usually among the French, is evidently that of the seventeenth century of Corneille and Racine. The drama of the sixteenth century does not handle plot in the same way as do these later artists. Therefore, he implies, it is worthless. Such an orientation toward the problems of literary criticism indicates a failure to discover a cardinal principle of criticism, to wit: There is no known body of critical principles that is capable of functioning to explain satisfactorily all art works of all periods. From this, it follows as a corollary that every period of art history and every individual work of art must be studied for what it is rather than for what it should have been. The sixteenth-century theater must be understood in the light of its own immanent principles. Attitudes of contempt or admiration are equally beside the point in arriving at such an understanding.

A remark by Lebègue concerning Jodelle's *Cléopâtre* runs to much the same effect as Lanson's observations and possesses the same degree of relevancy to the sixteenth-century theater and its artistic will. 'Autres défauts: le caractère des personnages n'est ni fouillé ni nuancé, aucune leçon morale ne se dégage nettement de ce fait-divers . . .' (Raymond Lebègue, *La tragédie française de la renaissance* [Brussels, 1944], p. 31.)

Another remark by Lebègue concerning Jodelle's *Cléopâtre* is of interest to the student as a further instance of the persistence into present-day criticism of the nineteenth-century concept of a universal esthetic standard to which all works must conform if they are to be awarded the official seal of approval. 'Pas d'incertitude, pas un conflit intérieur. Rien n'est plus vide.' (Lebègue, *La tragédie française*, p. 31.) These qualities that he regards as faults are rather to be considered part of the ideal toward which the playwright of that time strove.

⁶ Leonardo's 'Last Supper' (Fig. 12) typifies the general Renaissance habit of spreading the figures across the foreground. The organizing form in this instance is the table, which almost fills the frame and facilitates the arrangement of all the figures in the foremost plane parallel with the front of the picture. As is usual in a sixteenth-century painting, Christ, the most important one in the assembly, is seated in the center.

3
Garnier, *Hippolyte* (1573)[1]

SUMMARY OF PLOT AND PLOT SCHEME

ACT I

Scene i (pp. 247–51)—Aegeus sketches briefly the antecedents of the story that is to be presented and foretells Theseus' disgrace and the death of Phaedra and Hippolytus.

Scene ii (pp. 251–55)—Hippolytus relates a dream he has had in which a lion was about to kill him. He tells of other recent signs that are a portent of evil to come and asks the gods to preserve him from harm.

Scene iii (pp. 255–57)—The chorus of hunters enlarges on the pleasures of the chase and of the life of those who live by it.

ACT II

Scene i (pp. 258–76)—Phaedra complains of Theseus' long absence and of her burning love for Hippolytus. The Nurse urges her to overcome this shameful love, and her advice finally has sufficient effect so that Phaedra decides that suicide is the only honorable way of ending her dishonor. The Nurse is horrified and immediately promises to persuade Hippolytus to accept Phaedra's love.

Scene ii (pp. 276–78)—The chorus descants on the cruelty of love.

ACT III

Scene i (pp. 279–81)—Phaedra blames Cupid for her troubles. She begs the absent Hippolytus to be merciful and return her love, then leaves the stage.

Scene ii (pp. 281–83)—The nurse remarks on Phaedra's unpredictability and her rapidly changing attitudes brought on by the tortures of love.

Scene iii (pp. 283–84)—Phaedra returns, bewailing her misery, and accepts the nurse's suggestion that she pray to Diana. The nurse warns her that Hippolytus is approaching and Phaedra leaves the stage.

Scene iv (pp. 284–88)—The nurse tries to dispose Hippolytus favorably toward love but he rejects the idea and stalks out.

Scene v (pp. 288–90)—The nurse calls Phaedra on stage and tells her that Hippolytus will soon return.

Scene vi (pp. 290–96)—Phaedra tells Hippolytus that she is in love with him. He rejects her solicitations. She asks him to kill her but he refuses.

Scene vii (pp. 296–97)—The nurse enters and advises Phaedra to accuse Hippolytus and put all the blame on him.

Scene viii (pp. 297–99)—The chorus remarks on the rage of a woman scorned and makes a half-veiled prophecy that Phaedra's false accusations will bring her to ruin.

ACT IV

Scene i (p. 300)—Theseus announces his return from Hades.

Scene ii (pp. 300–302)—The nurse tells Theseus that Phaedra, for reasons unknown, is determined to kill herself.

Scene iii (pp. 302–309)—After Theseus threatens to torture the nurse, Phaedra tells him that Hippolytus has tried to make love to her. Theseus asks Neptune to kill Hippolytus.

Scene iv (pp. 309–11)—The nurse blames herself for the misery that has fallen on Theseus, Hippolytus, and Phaedra.

Scene v (pp. 311–13)—The chorus implores Neptune to consider the demands of justice rather than his vow to Theseus and to refrain from killing Hippolytus.

ACT V

Scene i (pp. 313–19)—A messenger enters and tells Theseus that his son is dead. He recites in detail how the event took place and Theseus indicates that his only regret is that he himself was responsible for it.

Scene ii (pp. 319–22)—Phaedra informs Theseus that her accusation was false, that Hippolytus was innocent, and that she is the guilty one. She goes out to kill herself.

Scene iii (pp. 322–24)—The chorus of Athenians expresses sorrow at the great evil that has come to their king and his family.

Scene iv (pp. 324–36)—Theseus bewails his misery and asks Diana to have him killed and eaten by a lion, since he does not deserve to die in a normal fashion and be buried.

PLOT

An examination of the summary of the plot indicates that the forms impressed upon it are still largely those of the Renaissance. The theme of the love of Phaedra for Hippolytus is the only plot, so that the concept of the fusion of a leading motive with minor ones does not arise. The prologue makes immediate reference to Phaedra's love and the fatal consequences it will have for Hippolytus. In each of the scenes that follow, including the choruses, the leading motive dominates, as it must in view of the absence of any other subject. This permanent governance of the single theme creates a feeling of inevitability concerning the course of the action. It is this feeling of the inescapable that insures in *Hippolyte* the Renaissance pattern of a slow and steady rise in tension until the death of Phaedra. For its full comprehension, all this must be viewed against the contrasting background of the later practices of the Baroque theater, which will often insist on developing emotional tension to a point of near-hysteria. The absence of any intent on the part of the Renaissance to exploit feeling in this extreme manner is epitomized in the management of Theseus' return from Hades in IV, i. No attempt has been made in the previous acts to create uncertainty or intense emotion of any kind concerning his appearance, and when he comes on stage he does so in the first scene of the act without fanfare. His return is evidently conceived as an event which is to be accepted casually and without thought of its value as an element of surprise. This is to be contrasted with Racine's treatment of the same incident in his *Phèdre*, where he thinks of the scene, insofar as its formal relations are concerned, in

terms that give prime consideration to the maximum shock value that
can be extracted from the situation. The stress that is produced in the
Renaissance theater arises as a consequence of the steady flow of events
toward the unavoidable catastrophe. There is as yet nothing in the play
now under examination of the desire for the irregularly fluctuating
tension of mystery that will come to typify the work of the high Baroque.
This is evident in Phaedra's blunt statement that she is in love with
Hippolytus. In II, i (p. 260), she says:

> ô quatre fois mauditte
> La flèche que tu pris dans les yeux d'Hippolyte,
> D'Hippolyte que j'aime, et non pas seulement
> Que j'aime, mais de qui j'enrage follement.

In V, i (p. 314), the messenger tells of Hippolytus' death in terms that
are equally direct: 'Hippolyte (ô regret!) vient de perdre la vie.' This
statement evidently corresponds to the wish for a complete clarity. It
must be noted, however, that when the messenger first appears and
seems to be ready to tell what everyone has already inferred, he still
delays the actual communication for several speeches. Here, the author
is working under the governance of a determination to interrupt the
easy flow of an absolutely clear plot for the sake of building up tension
by means of hesitation. The messenger's speeches, therefore, afford an
instance of the interpenetration of the formal prepossessions of the
Renaissance with those of the rising new esthetic.

Within the framework of the one plot, each scene functions as a
separate unit. This will be made clear by an analysis of Acts I and III,
the parts in which this autonomy is perhaps most apparent in this play.

In Act I, scene i, Aegeus delivers the prologue, which summarizes the
action of the play. In scene ii, Hippolytus recounts a dream and a number of experiences that have led him to conceive some ill-defined fears
regarding his possible death. In scene iii, the chorus of hunters dwells on
the happiness of the men who live by the chase. The subject matter of
each division is so clearly marked that each can be given its own title,

as follows: Scene i, introduction and summary of the story; scene ii, Hippolytus' fears; scene iii, the pleasures of the chase. There is no hint here of the later technique of introducing a scene that dangles, with its relations to the rest of the plot completely obscure, until it is picked up and continued later in the play.

Act III, scene i is a monolog of complaint and supplication by Phaedra. Scene ii is a monolog by the nurse concerning Phaedra's unhappiness. In scene iii, the two meet for a brief talk before Hippolytus enters; their conversation serves as an introduction for the following scene. In iv, the nurse tries to dispose Hippolytus favorably toward the idea of love but he contemptuously rejects her advice. In v, the nurse calls Phaedra in and tells her that Hippolytus will soon appear. Scene vi contains Phaedra's confession of love and her rejection by Hippolytus. In scene vii, the nurse advises Phaedra to accuse Hippolytus. Scene viii is devoted to the remarks of the chorus concerning Phaedra's rage and the lack of wisdom in her determination to accuse Hippolytus. Each scene moves tranquilly through its assigned subject matter and ends with a few words or lines that have the sound of a closing cadence. The scene that follows enters upon a different subject, exploits it to the desired extent, and ends again with a phrase that has the usual air of finality. An examination of the plot scheme indicates that this analysis holds true of most and perhaps all of the remaining scenes of *Hippolyte*.

At the same time that each scene is relatively independent, all are held together by a strong central motive that acts effectively to hold the separate parts together in a close unity. This procedure, by which a number of self-contained units are dominated and unified by a single theme that is not found in its entirety in any one scene, can be more fully understood if it is contrasted with the Baroque technique. In the Baroque theater, the plot does not consist of scenes that cluster around an overriding motive, but rather of a number of subplots whose relation to the main theme is not at first apparent. As a matter of fact, it regularly happens in the Baroque drama of both Spain and France that the identity of the leading theme is not made clear until the play is well advanced.

9. Raphael: School of Athens

10. Pieter Brueghel the Elder: Hunters in the Snow

11. Titian: Venus of Urbino

12. Leonardo da Vinci: The Last Supper

A single illustration will suffice to elucidate the present manner of attaining the unity that is indispensable to any work of art. In Act II, there are only two scenes, one consisting of the conversation between Phaedra and the nurse, the other of a chant by the chorus on the cruelty of love. The separate nature of each scene is apparent, while at the same time it is evident that the general motive of Phaedra's love ties them together. This manner of disposing scenes in succession along the sole line of action is analogous to the arrangement of the receding distance in a series of parallel planes in sixteenth-century painting, and gives a similar effect of tranquility and inevitability.[2] In both cases, the existence of a common artistic method is apparent. In Garnier's play, unity of plot seems to have been attained in a manner typical of the Renaissance.

The acts are handled in the same way as the scenes. Each one deals with its assigned portion of the story, passes through a closing cadence, and comes to a slow, majestic conclusion in the speech of the chorus. This is true of all the acts except the last, in which a closing speech by Theseus is attached after the chorus speaks. The formal objective throughout is not to create uncertainty concerning the action but rather to present a series of tranquil, sonorous declamations grouped about the tragedy of Phaedra's love, conduct it with a slow rhythm to a foreseen conclusion, and then come to an ending of august dignity. All these qualities imply that there is in the present case a wish to conduct the developing action along a single line of plot to a clearly anticipated ending. This wish constantly makes itself felt throughout the play, as it does in III, vii (p. 296) and viii (pp. 297–99). In scene vii, the nurse advises Phaedra to accuse Hippolytus of her own sin, while, in scene viii, the chorus descants on the lengths to which a jealous, revengeful woman will go. The author's intention is to suggest, before the actual event, that she will accuse him. It is to be noted, however, that the author pushes certainty in this matter only to the point of strong suggestion; here, as elsewhere, the will to a relentless march along a settled line of action no longer goes to the point of flat, open assertion in a few words. In this matter, an incipient will to the uncertain is making itself felt.

E

This compounding of Rennaissance and Baroque occurs also in the prologue spoken by Aegeus. The story of incest, death, and suffering is foretold and Hippolytus' death is prophesied. The manner of telling, however, is such that the outcome remains doubtful to a certain degree. In no case is there an unequivocal assertion in a few words that these events will occur. The technique is rather one of lengthy hint and suggestion that avoid the brief, direct statement. Hippolytus' coming death is stated in these uncertain terms (I, i, p. 250):

> Las! Je te voy meurtry par cette Minoïde,
> (Si quelque bon Démon aujourd'huy ne te guide) . . .

In I, ii (pp. 254–55), Hippolytus says of his vague fears of impending disaster:

> C'est en vain, c'est en vain: tout cela n'a puissance
> De faire révoquer la céleste ordonnance.
>
> .   .   .   .
>
> Amorty ces frayeurs qui me glacent les veines,
> O Délienne, et fay qu'elles demeurent vaines!
> Recule tout désastre et accident mauvais
> Loing de moy, ma déesse, et loing de ce palais!

In the first two lines of this speech, the author, guided by a feeling for inevitability, gives a clear indication of the course the story is to follow; Hippolytus' efforts to avoid the ordained flow of events will be useless. But this close adherence to the single line of plot is vitiated to a certain degree by the remarks that follow, which indicate that Hippolytus himself has no idea of the nature of this impending disaster and hopes to avoid it. This insignificant deviation from the clear definition of the sole motive is indicative of a new feeling for the treatment of plot. The Renaissance proper would have felt no need for even the mild disturbance introduced here by way of the uneasiness of one of the chief actors over fears that are vague and formless.

In III, vi (p. 291), Hippolytus says to Phaedra, 'Ma mère, fiez-vous à moy de vos ennemis.' The reference to Phaedra as his mother is included in order to heighten the feeling of horror at Phaedra's incestuous love. In addition, it makes clear that Hippolytus has no suspicion of what Phaedra is preparing to say and puts the audience into a flutter of almost morbid anticipation in their wish to see what his reaction will be when she discloses her illegitimate affection. This feeling, which depends on the extreme emotional strain created by the absence of any sure knowledge of what Hippolytus will do, constitutes a sharp deviation from the Renaissance inevitability of plot. This same tendency to deflect the action from a conclusion that is in other places prophesied is apparent in III, viii (p. 299). The chorus recalls that many other ancient heroes have been in danger of their lives, just as Hippolytus now is. The concluding stanza is as follows:

> Mais s'il y a là haut encore
> Quelque déité qu'on adore
> S'il y a des dieux ayans soing
> D'assister les bons au besoing,
> Ils permettront que la malice,
> Contre ta vertu rebouchant,
> Recherra dessur son authrice,
> Bourreau de son crime méchant.

This suggests another possible course of action than the one that is actually to be followed and constitutes a relatively mild divergence from the single plot that is not at all characteristic of a Renaissance treatment. Beneath the predominant feeling of inevitability, there is constantly at work an undercurrent of doubt concerning the direction the plot will take.

Another divergence from the easily flowing single plot occurs in the last scene of the play (p. 325), where Theseus blames himself for not committing suicide:

> Sus, que tardes-tu donc? une crainte couarde
> Te rend elle plus mol que ta femme paillarde?
> . . . .

> Non, tu ne dois mourir . . .
>
> .   .   .   .
>
> Mais si, tu dois mourir . . .

Theseus' vacillation between two lines of conduct signifies the disappearance of the majestic singleness of purpose that is typical of the Renaissance hero. The tortured indecision of Baroque man before the problems of life is beginning to appear and the reduction of the monumental personality of the tragic hero to the dimensions of the intimately human is progressing.

The larger outline of the plot is managed in a typically Renaissance fashion. As the previous evidence suggests, a logical development is deliberately sought; that is, the author wants the course of the story to be made clear at the beginning and he is interested in giving frequent assurances that this course is being held to closely. In the opening scene, Aegeus furnishes a brief summary of the story that is to be presented, so condensed that it is compressed into only three or four lines. He says in an apostrophe to Theseus (p. 250):

> Tu occiras, meurtrier, ta propre géniture,
> Puis l'adultère mort de ta femme parjure
> Doublera tes ennuis . . .

Here, the plot is revealed completely and there is a manifest desire to proceed logically. The same wish motivates a speech by Hippolytus in I, ii (p. 254):

> Mais quoy? rien ne se change; on a beau faire voeux,
> On a beau immoler des centaines de boeufs,
> C'est en vain, c'est en vain: tout cela n'a puissance
> De faire révoquer la céleste ordonnance.

In II, i (p. 271), Phaedra says in reference to her struggle against her love for Hippolytus:

> Mais toujours à la fin Amour est le vaincueur,
> Qui paisible du camp s'empare de mon cueur.

This constitutes an assurance to the audience that she will not be able to conquer her passion and that the story will continue in the path that has been marked out for it. In II, i (p. 276), the nurse says of Hippolytus:

> Il nous faut aborder cet homme solitaire,
> Et tâcher d'amollir son naturel sévère:
> Cela sera ma charge.

This future plot development is outlined well in advance and assures the spectators that the story is evolving along the lines that have already been laid down. In the constant recurrence of these technical devices, the author manifests a devotion to an esthetic in which surprise is rather to be avoided than sought out. Another signal that functions to affirm that the original plan is still being used occurs in III, vi (p. 296), where the nurse says to Phaedra:

> Nostre faute est cogneuë: et bien, et bien, mon âme,
> Il faut le prévenir et luy donner le blâme,
> Accusons-le luy-mesme . . .

In the scene that follows (pp. 297–99), the entire chant of the chorus serves, insofar as the form is concerned, as a channel to aid in guiding the plot along its previously determined course. In this case, the reference to the fury of a jealous woman lends additional certainty that Phaedra will go through with the proposed accusation of Hippolytus.

So pervasive is the felt need for logical development in Garnier's *Hippolyte* that guide posts are set up even where they seem to be superfluous. The opening lines of Act V are as follows (p. 313):

> Messager
> O la triste adventure! ô le malheureux sort!
> O desastre! ô mechef! ô déplorable mort!
> Thésée
> Il parle d'Hippolyte.

By this time, the situation has evolved so far and in such a way that the messenger's lines can refer only to Hippolytus. Even where the allusion is obvious, however, the comprehensive will of the Renaissance artist to meet the demands of a logical form impels the author in the present case to state briefly what has already been inferred. The same esthetic prepossessions lie behind the last two lines spoken by Phaedra in V, ii (p. 322):

> Il est temps de mourir; sus, que mon sang ondoye
> Sur ce corps trespassé, courant d'une grand' playe.

By now her suicide is inescapable, but the desire for a constant guidance of the plot in its fixed channel dictates this brief statement to the effect that her death is now imminent.

At the same time that the handling of the plot in its large outline is characteristic of the Renaissance technique, a new tendency to avoid a visibly logical development makes its appearance in a number of smaller details. In I, ii (p. 252), in Hippolytus' description of his dream, the sudden appearance of the lion lends an effect of dramatic surprise that proceeds from the abruptness of its presentation, without any previous suggestion of what is to come. In regard to this same scene (p. 254), mention has already been made of the inevitability implied in Hippolytus' remark concerning his fate, 'Mais quoy? rien ne se change . . .' This attitude of assurance concerning the plot, however, is accompanied by the uncertainty that is lent by Hippolytus' ignorance of precisely what fate awaits him, as well as the hint that Diana may yet rescue him from the mysterious evil that impends. This suggestion is contained in the last two lines of his soliloquy (p. 255):

> Recule tout désastre et accident mauvais
> Loing de moy, ma déesse, et loing de ce palais!

In III, vi (pp. 290–94), the smooth flow of the story from one fore-ordained event to the next is interrupted by the rather long delay in

Phaedra's confession to Hippolytus that she is in love with him. In keeping with the new attitudes that are arising, her declaration hangs on the
edge for a hundred lines or so, threatening to break over at any moment
but held up by repeated delays. The audience has been told in advance
what Phaedra will have to say to him, but the procedures of the Renaissance technique are no longer completely satisfactory to Garnier. The
Renaissance proper would not have thought in terms of such a roundabout approach to an incident. It would have tended to treat the whole
situation as settled and known in advance, and would not have presented it in this halting, hesitating fashion. This temporary break in the
continuity of the action is new both in the form (delay and hesitation)
and in the emotional tone that grows out of this form (tension and intimate, non-heroic feeling). When Phaedra's avowal of love is finally
made, it takes an indirect form. In the lines beginning 'L'amour con-
somme enclos . . .' (III, vi, p. 293), she refers to her love for Hippolytus
in such a way that he assumes that she is speaking of Theseus. In her
next speech beginning 'Hélas! voire, Hippolyte . . .' (pp. 293–94), she
describes Hippolytus under the pretense of referring to Theseus. Here
and at other places in the scene, her words have a double meaning, of
which Hippolytus perceives only the more innocent part. This piquant
vagueness will continue to recommend itself to the authors of the high
Baroque because it half reveals while at the same time it withholds a
full disclosure. The audience can enjoy the delicate emotional titillation
of understanding the situation completely and of seeing Hippolytus on
the verge of discovery, with only a thin veil between himself and
Phaedra's secret. Even the actual declaration is indirect. Instead of saying openly, 'Je t'aime' or 'J'aime Hippolyte,' she says, '. . . et moy
j'aime le fils.' This constitutes a full-blown will to indirection, for partial concealment and sudden revelation, which still operate within the
general desire to conform with the demands of a logical manipulation
of the plot.

    This same predilection for a roundabout approach to specific points
of plot delineation motivates Phaedra's delay in accusing Hippolytus
of making love to her. In IV, iii (p. 305), she says to Theseus, 'Je vous

conteray tout . . .' The accusation, however, instead of following at
once, is made only after several additional speeches. When it finally
emerges, it is stated with the same indirectness with which Phaedra
makes her avowal of love to Hippolytus. Instead of saying bluntly that
Hippolytus is the one responsible for her sorrow, she says (p. 306):

> Ce coutelas tranchant
> Qu'il laissa de frayeur au bruit du populaire
> Le voyant vous fera connoistre l'adultère.

The avoidance of the name of the accused and the conveyance of it by
reference to his sword are indicative of a tendency toward delay and
indirection that constitute a running accompaniment to the lucid plot
development that characterizes the present play.

STYLE

In many respects, the style is typical of the Renaissance. The verse is
regular, with few run-on lines and with the main caesura located, in
most cases, at the sixth syllable; that is, it adheres to logical patterns of
expression. The figures of speech also are often characteristic of the
Renaissance, as is the case with Phaedra's comparison of her unhappy
state with that of a ship in a storm, in II, i (p. 271):

> Ainsi voit-on souvent une nef passagère
> Au milieu de la mer, quand elle se colère,
> Ne pouvoir aborder, tant un contraire vent
> Seigneuriant les flots le bat par le devant.
> Les nochers esperdus ont beau caler les voiles,
> Ont beau courir au mast, le désarmer de toiles,
> Ont beau coucher la rame, et de tout leur effort
> Tâcher malgré le vent de se traîner au port,
> Leur labeur n'y fait rien: la mugissante haleine
> Du nort, qui les repousse, anéantist leur peine,
> La nef court eslancée, ou contre quelque banc,
> Ou contre quelque roc, qui luy brise le flanc.

The metaphor is typical of the Renaissance—direct, somewhat conventional, and involving a comparison that is easily understood and has nothing of the bizarre. There is no hint here of the 'conceit' later defined by Baltasar Gracián as an artificial, startling, and even far-fetched connection between two highly disparate objects.[3] Another figure of this kind occurs in a speech by Phaedra in III, i (p. 281), where she refers to her unhappiness:

> Voyez-vous pas sortir comme d'une fournaise
> Les soupirs de ma bouche aussi chauds comme braise?

Other such conventional metaphors are easy to find. In III, iii (p. 284), Phaedra prays to Diana to help her win Hippolytus:

> Ouvre le coeur glacé d'Hippolyte, et luy mets
> Les tisons de l'amour dans ses os enflamez . . .

In III, v (p. 289), the nurse remarks on Hippolytus' imperviousness to her pleas on behalf of Phaedra:

> Je ne le voy non plus esmeu de mes propos
> Qu'un grand roc rivager n'est esbranlé des flots.

In V, i (p. 316), the messenger compares the great bull that killed Hippolytus to the sky during a summer storm:

> Comme quand en esté le ciel se courrouçant
> Noircist, esclaire, bruit, les hommes menaçant . . .

The figures here are all conventional, indicating that the Renaissance had no stronger predilection for surprises in style than in plot or character.

At the same time that Garnier's technique in the rendition of the metaphor is permeated with a Renaissance spirit, it is also often touched by the new feeling for the treatment of linguistic forms. In I, i (p. 250), Aegeus refers to the sufferings that Theseus will have to endure:

Jà desjà je te voy porter l'affliction
De quelque Promethée ou de quelque Ixion,
D'un Tantale altéré, d'un remangé Titye,
D'un Typhon, d'un Sisyphe, et si l'horreur noircie
De Pluton garde encore un plus aspre tourment,
L'on t'en ira gesner perpétuellement.

The enumeration of a large number of parallels to Theseus' affliction seems to be indicative of the growing predilection for exuberance of form, an outlook that attains full expression in such well-known manifestations of the high Baroque as the profuse surface decoration of the architecture of that period.[4] A striking parallel with the painting of the time can be observed in this same scene (p. 250), where Aegeus recounts the tortures that will be visited on Theseus after his death:

Le sévère Minos et le cruel Pluton,
Tous deux tes outragez, hucheront Alecton,
Mégère, Tisiphone, exécrables bourrelles,
Pour ribler, forcener, ravager en tes moüelles,
T'élancer leurs serpens en cent plis renouez
T'ardre de leurs flambeaux, et de leurs rouges fouets,
Te battre dos et ventre, aussi dru que la gresle
Craquetant, bondissant, découpe un épi gresle.

The description here is highly detailed, grim, intensely physical, and gory, and is strictly parallel in these respects to the painting of a scene of martyrdom by Rubens. In both cases, the intent is to impress the spectator with the physical horror of the situation, to attain a maximum vividness, and to draw the spectator into a personal, intimate participation in the scene depicted. This same wish to encourage the audience to take part in the action lies behind the detailed description of Hippolytus' fears in I, ii (pp. 251–55).

One other example will suffice, along with those already adduced, to illustrate the stylistic transformation that is taking place at this time (1573). The rather extravagant praise of Hippolytus by Phaedra is a case in point. In III, i (p. 280), she says:

> Je ne croy pas aussi, tithonienne Aurore,
> Que tu baises le sein de ton Céphale encore :
> Au moins si quelquefois en respandant le jour,
> Baissant les yeux à bas, tu as veu mon amour.

This hyperbolic language is a distant prophecy of the extremes to which Baroque taste will go in the course of the seventeenth century. This growing extravagance of language is matched by and goes along with the increasingly desperate quality of emotional tension that will later have issue in the Baroque tendency toward the hysterical in art.

The language throughout the play is pitched on a dignified and elevated level. The emotional quality is by turns quiet and restrained, in Renaissance fashion, and extravagant, after an incipient Baroque manner. In this connection I, i (the prologue by Aegeus), with its somber restraint, can be contrasted with the stronger feeling of III, i (Phaedra's soliloquy on her unhappiness). A further contrast between the practices of the Renaissance and the Baroque is visible in a remark by Theseus in IV, i (p. 301). In remarking on his astonishment at his cool reception, he says, 'Est-ce un deuil fait exprès / Pour me mieux recevoir me sçachant icy près?' This, the sole touch of humor in the play, anticipates the later use of humor in the serious drama of the high Baroque, especially in the Spanish *comedia*. Even this almost imperceptible humor is in sharp contrast with the uniform seriousness of the preceding tragedies of the Renaissance. At the same time that it is a mark of the drift away from the ideals of the earlier period, it is also an indication of the distance yet to be traveled before the transfer to the attitudes of the seventeenth century shall be complete. It is this new position that will give rise, in France and elsewhere, to the invention of the tragi-comedy, the pre-eminent vehicle for the expression of modern sentiments in regard to the drama as an art.

The Renaissance mode of handling opposed ideas is epitomized in part of a speech by Phaedra in III, i (p. 279). She says:

> Hé! dieux, qu'y faut-il faire? Hippolyte m'espoint,
> Et quand il est présent et quand il n'y est point.

Garnier, still working under the influence of the Renaissance ideal, fails to play up the contrast of ideas by putting it in parallel structural forms. The same manner of treating opposite ideas occurs as well in a pair of lines spoken by Hippolytus (I, ii, p. 251):

> O beau soleil luisant, belle et claire planette,
> Qui pousses tes rayons dedans la nuict brunette . . .

In other cases, however, contrasted ideas are expressed in a formal pattern that approximates to those of the Baroque. In IV, ii (pp. 301–302), the discussion by Theseus and the nurse concerning Phaedra's unhappiness is cast in the typical pattern of paired lines that express opposed concepts.

Thésée

Qui peut à mon retour causer ce déconfort?

Nourrice

C'est pour votre retour qu'elle haste sa mort.

Thésée

Elle veut donc mourir pour me revoir en vie?

Nourrice

Non, mais votre retour luy en accroist l'envie.

Thésée

Prend elle desplaisir que je soy' revenu?

Nourrice

Vostre absence luy est un regret continu.

Thésée

Qui luy cause la mort sçachant bien ma présence?

Nourrice

Je ne sçay, mais je voy que c'est ce qui l'offence.

Thésée

Quelle nouvelle rage est entrée en son coeur?

Nourrice

Un despit qui la ronge, une triste langueur.

In the scene that follows (pp. 303–304), the antithesis is expressed in both one-line and two-line passages whose parallelism of structure points up the contrast of ideas:

Thésée
Quelle cause vous meut de désirer la mort?

Phèdre
Si je vous la disois, je périrois à tort,
Et le fruict périroit que de la mort j'espère.

Thésée
Ne le dites qu'à moy: je le sçauray bien taire.

Phèdre
Ce qu'on veut que quelcun taise fidellement,
Le faut soymesme taire: il est sceu autrement.

Thésée
Mais un loyal mary vers sa femme qu'il aime
N'est pas un estranger, c'est un autre elle mesme.

Phèdre
Une femme ne doit conter à son mary
Chose dont il puisse estre en le sçachant marry.

Thésée
Que me peut-on conter, qui plus de deuil me cause
Que de vous voir mourir sans en sçavoir la cause?

Phèdre
Si de me voir mourir vous prenez quelque esmoy,
Il n'amoindrira pas quand vous sçaurez pourquy.

Thésée
Que me peut proffiter ceste tristesse teue?

Phèdre
Que vous peut proffiter ceste tristesse sceue?

Thésée
On remédie au mal quand on le peut sçavoir.

Phèdre
A celuy que j'endure il n'y a point d'espoir.

Thésée
Que vous sert donc la mort, de tous les maux le pire?

Phèdre
La mort fait terminer tout angoisseux martyre.

Additional illustrations of this Baroque attitude toward opposed ideas set in similar formal patterns can be observed in Phaedra's argument with the nurse in II, i (pp. 261–62 and 264–65).

The often intimate and even extravagant emotional atmosphere of Garnier's *Hippolyte* has already been referred to. One of the contributing factors to this deviation from the dignified restraint and reserve of the Renaissance is the repetition of a word or phrase, a technical recourse that occurs with some frequency in this work. A typical instance is found in Phaedra's soliloquy in II, i (p. 258), where, in an apostrophe to her native island of Crete, she says:

> Pourquoy, mon cher séjour, mon cher séjour, pourquoy
> M'as-tu de toy bannie en éternel esmoy?

In another of Phaedra's soliloquies, in III, i (p. 279), she says in an apostrophe to Hippolytus:

> Je meurs de vous trop voir! je meurs, hélas! je meurs
> De vous voir, ô beautez, semences de mes pleurs!

In this same scene (p. 280), she says, 'Où courez-vous, mon coeur? mon coeur, où courez-vous?' And in V, ii (p. 322), the author makes use of this device in Phaedra's farewell:

> Adieu, soleil luisant, soleil luisant, adieu!
> Adieu, triste Thésée! adieu, funèbre lieu!

Repetitions of this nature, which recur constantly throughout the play, indicate to what an extent the style of dramatic poetry has by this time (1573) diverged from that of the Renaissance, under which an emotional repetition of this kind was not so much frowned upon as simply not yet conceived as a stylistic possibility.

Along with these continuing transmutations of esthetic positions in regard to the management of plot, character, and language, there occurs at the same time a change of ideology. The struggle between virtue and evil has acquired a domestic, everyday flavor quite at variance with the elevated, heroic, impersonal flavor of the Renaissance tragedy. Garnier's *Hippolyte* is largely concerned with the struggle in Phaedra's soul between two moral principles, one that is good (faithfulness in marriage) and one that is evil (incestuous free love). There seems to be nothing left of the impersonal and unequal struggle between destiny and the gods on the one hand, and a weak and helpless mortal on the other. This would appear to proceed from the tendency, already mentioned, to make art more intimate by persuading the spectator to take a more active part in it. Like the plastic arts contemporaneous with Garnier's play, the drama is becoming more domestic and intimate, that is, it is growing in the direction of the Baroque.

The language in the present play contributes its part to the creation of a work that generally follows the older logical tradition, although the numerous reservations already suggested must be kept in mind. The manner of handling a figure of speech will make this clear. In II, i (p. 271), Phaedra compares herself to a ship in a storm that tries to make port and fails. The author is not content to leave the connection of even this easy, conventional trope to the imagination of the audience. Immediately after the metaphor is brought to an end, Garnier states its application to Phaedra:

> Ainsi cette fureur violente s'oppose
> A ce que la raison salutaire propose . . .

Although the style is often, and perhaps usually, clear and logical, examples of a new tendency are not lacking. In I, ii (p. 251), Hippolytus describes his dream as follows:

> Il me sembloit, dormant, que j'erroy solitaire
> Au creux d'une forest, mon esbat ordinaire,
> Descendu dans un val, que mille arbres autour,
> Le ceinturant espois, privent de nostre jour.
> Il y faisoit obscur, mais non pas du tout comme
> En une pleine nuict qu'accompagne le somme,
> Mais comme il fait au soir, après que le soleil

A retiré de nous son visage vermeil,
Et qu'il relaisse encore une lueur qui semble
Estre ny jour ny nuict, mais tous les deux ensemble.

This depiction of an indeterminate landscape seen in a dim, mysterious light is not characteristic of the Renaissance. The sixteenth century was interested in the clear and perfectly visible, and had not yet conceived of the esthetic possibilities inherent in a landscape that was half dark and half light. The parallel with painting in both the sixteenth and seventeenth centuries is evident enough.[5] The softly emotional tone of this entire scene in Garnier's work, the interest in the twilight zone of the subconcious, the uneasy mystery of Hippolytus' misgivings regarding some disaster, the dark, half-seen menace of hooting owls and howling dogs, all denote a gravitation toward a new species of clarity. The brooding obscurity that pervades this portion of the play is far removed from the clear, open quality of a Renaissance work, where action and motives are deliberately laid out for the audience to see and where the only concern is with the external elements of a conventional psychology. This delving into the lower levels of the mind would have seemed morbid and unhealthy to the artists of forty years before but is gradually coming to have a fascination for the advocates of the new art.

On the basis of the data that have been recorded and the inferences that have been drawn from them, it is possible to venture the observation that Garnier's *Hippolyte* still clings to the fundamental tenets of the Renaissance drama but that it also possesses a number of relatively advanced qualities that show a marked trend toward the Baroque; these qualities are thoroughly blended with the conservative traits of the preceding period into a work that is typical of the intermediate period to which it belongs.

CHARACTERS

The admixture of Renaissance forms with those of a new school of artistic thought is as manifest in the conception of character as in the

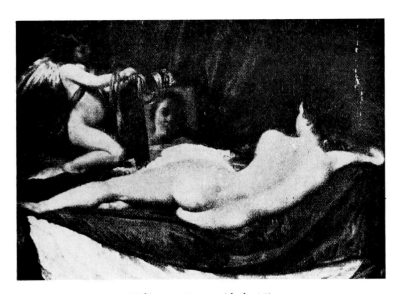

13. Velásquez: Venus with the Mirror

14. Hans Holbein the Younger: Edward VI when Prince of Wales

15. Poussin: Triumph of Flora

management of plot and style. Hippolytus' scornful attitude toward
women is maintained throughout the play. This conception of personality can be better understood if Garnier's Hippolytus is compared
with Racine's. In keeping with his wish to saturate his work with the
tenderness of love, Racine causes Hippolytus to fall in love with Aricia.
In Garnier's play, as far as love is concerned, Hippolytus is still the
intractable Renaissance hero, stubbornly devoted to his single-minded
detestation of women.

In another respect, however, the conception of the hero has undergone a change. Hippolytus is no longer the majestic, monumental hero
of the preceding period, but is closer to the ordinary mortal, with all
the fears and feelings to which he is subject. Garnier's Phaedra is similar
but has gravitated still closer to the Baroque heroine; she is changeable
and hysterically devoted to her love, which at times completely sub-
merges her sense of duty and honor. In Act I and part of Act II, she is
dominated by her passion for Hippolytus and is determined to have
him regardless of the consequences. In II, i (p. 274), she sees the error
of her way and resolves to kill herself. In III, i (pp. 279–81), she is again
determined to have him if it is possible. These rapid, violent changes of
intention and outlook are quite different from the static, unchanging
moral positions that characterize the Renaissance personality as it is
expressed in the theater. The nervous excitability of the Baroque
heroine, so different from the calm march of the Renaissance heroine
to her fate, is epitomized in III, i (p. 281), where the nurse says:

> Elle va forcenée, ores pour s'outrager,
> Ores pleine d'espoir se semble encourager.

This constitutes a probably unconscious expression of the new
orientation before the problem of the rendition of dramatic character
that was rapidly growing up in the tragedy. For the Renaissance, personality was rigid and stable; for the Baroque, it will often be fluid and
unstable. These transformations of attitude will become common in
the theater of the high Baroque (1600–1650), and can be illustrated in

F

the sudden change in Segismundo's nature in Calderón's *La vida es sueño* (1635) and the vacillation of Chimène between duty and love in Corneille's *Le Cid* (1637). In the case of Phaedra, there is a notable drift toward the emotional intimacy that will become a settled part of the Baroque conception of character in the theater. In her complaint concerning her unhappiness in II, i (pp. 258–60), for example, the spectator is led to enter into her most secret feelings and to experience them as though they were his own. The tone is soft and plaintive, and is quite unlike the unyielding march of the Renaissance heroine to her doom. It should not be inferred that the intimateness and emotional softness referred to are strictly limited to those passages that have been cited. On the contrary, these attitudes inform the character of Phaedra throughout the play, although they are found in Hippolytus only now and then. In brief, Phaedra seems to be modeled after a new conception of the tragic heroine, while Hippolytus was created in accordance with an ideal of the hero that is still mostly but not entirely conservative in its dependence on the older attitude of the Renaissance.

Only four of the personages are of major importance—Hippolytus, Phaedra, the nurse, and Theseus. It is significant of the Renaissance simplicity in manipulating the story that no more than two characters are on the stage in any given scene. The relationships between the various personages adhere in general to the Renaissance pattern. The nurse, for example, participates in a single, unchanging relationship with Phaedra. She is designed to revolve about Phaedra and to minister unceasingly to her dominant role, with the single possible exception of her gravitation to the foreground when she suddenly changes her mind and decides to help her mistress capture Hippolytus. When she appears on stage with Theseus or Hippolytus, she acts always only to point to Phaedra and recall to the audience her mistress' paramount part in the play. At no time is she allowed to step out of this subsidiary function and reveal her own independent personality, except for the doubtful instance that has been mentioned. The difference between the sixteenth and seventeenth centuries in this respect may be better understood by referring to the momentary disclosure of the personality of such minor figures as Clarín in Calderón's *La vida es sueño* (I, iv, ll. 364–65; III, i, ll. 2188–2227) and Ortuño and Flores in Lope's *Fuenteovejuna* (I, ll. 627–34). The relations between all the other characters of *Hippolyte* are of the same rigid, exclusive nature as that between the nurse and Phaedra, with one notable exception. Phaedra and Hippolytus participate in a double connection that constantly shifts and refuses to fall into the stiff pattern that governs the other personages. In III, vi (p. 291), this exchange takes place between them:

> Hippolyte
> Ma mère, fiez-vous à moy de vos ennemis.
> Phèdre
> Laissez ce nom de mère, Hippolyte . . .

A few lines below (p. 292) Hippolytus returns to this supposed relationship that is so distasteful to Phaedra:

> Je prendray le souci de vos enfans, mes frères,
> Et vous honoreray, comme celle qui est
> De mon père l'espouse . . .

They are ostensibly stepmother and stepson, or, as it is phrased in order to make Phaedra's incestuous attraction seem more hideous, mother and son. It is necessary to the development of the given plot that this relationship should change to that of lovers. It is not, however, equally necessary that there should be a verbal insistence on this equivocal, uneasy relation. The author is intent on suggesting and emphasizing the uncertainty of the situation of the protagonists by insisting on the dual connection that subsists between them to such a point that it becomes ambiguous. A further formal purpose of this uneasy state of affairs is to be found in the emotional effect it exercises on the audience. In consonance with the growing demand for an extreme exploitation of feeling, the author is intent on wringing out of this explosive set of circumstances the maximum emotional effect.[6]

The nurse shows something of the same changeableness. The sudden transformation of her attitude, from one of condemnation of Phaedra's love to one of approval and even to a determination to help her, points toward the Baroque. The Renaissance would have expected, as a matter of course, that the nurse would run true to form throughout the play. The concept of personality is changing from static to dynamic; under the high Baroque, there will be a tendency to think of the individual as one who proceeds to an ultimate condition through various vicissitudes. Rather than 'being' in a single fixed state, character will 'become.'

The ambiguous way of dealing with Hippolytus and Phaedra is indicative of a new conception of relationships between characters. In other respects, the treatment of personality appears to be thoroughly Renaissance. The relation of principals and subsidiary persons is determined by a feeling for rigid compartmentalization, according to which each one is assigned to a place in a hierarchy that runs from high to low, and from which no deviation is permitted, with the one possible exception in the case of the nurse that has been alluded to. It follows from this that no connections are allowed to develop between secondary personages. Because of these rigidly exclusive relations, the two principal characters, Hippolytus and Phaedra, seem to be sharply detached from each other, and, in spite of being thrown into close association in a common tragedy, their lives and attitudes are highly disparate both in ideas and emotions. These limitations will come to seem excessive and artificial to the Baroque, whose answer to the demands for a new esthetic will be the creation of the tragi-comedy, which will differ from the tragedy not merely in the remission of the former attitudes toward the delineation of the characters and the connections between them but in many other formal aspects as well.

Notes

[1] The edition used is as follows: Robert Garnier, *Oeuvres complètes (théâtre et poésies) de Robert Garnier*, ed. Lucien Pinvert (Paris, 1923), I, 239–326. The play is divided into acts but not into scenes. The division into scenes is by the present writer. Subsequent references to *Hippolyte* are to this edition and will be indicated only by giving the act, scene, or page number. The lines of the play are not numbered in the edition cited.

[2] Titian's 'Venus of Urbino' (Fig. 11) can serve as an epitome of the Renaissance tendency to organize a picture in a series of planes that are parallel to the frame. The first plane is occupied by the reclining figure of Venus, while the second is represented by the wall on the left. The middle distance recedes in carefully organized steps over a floor whose clearly marked squares constitute a part of the meticulous articulation of parts. The wall in the right background furnishes another definite stop for the eye, which is then permitted to continue through the window to the tree and on beyond it to the background of the sky. The governing ideal in the organization of the picture space is one of careful control of receding space by means of a series of planes that are parallel to the frame.

[3] 'Consiste, pues este artificio conceptuoso en una primorosa concordancia, en una armónica correlación entre dos o tres conoscibles extremos, expresada por un acto del entendimiento . . . De suerte, que se puede definir el concepto. Es un acto del entendimiento, que exprime la correspondencia que se halla entre los objetos.' (Baltasar Gracián y Morales, *Agudeza y arte de ingenio* ['Biblioteca de filósofos españoles,' directed by Eduardo Ovejero y Maury] Madrid, 1929, p. 6.)

[4] This liking for luxuriant decoration is exemplified in the interior of the church of Wies in Upper Bavaria (Fig. 4), which may be contrasted with the austere plainness of the Palazzo della Cancelleria (Fig. 5).

[5] The extreme differences between light and dark in Rembrandt's 'Man with Golden Helmet' (Fig. 6) is in strong contrast with the Renaissance striving for clarity at every point. The bright light on the helmet stands out sharply against the shadowy background. Even the face is dim beside this brilliant spot of gold. This mode of handling light can be more fully comprehended if it is contrasted with the limpid clearness and uniformly diffused light that were universally preferred during the Renaissance. (See Fig. 1.)

[6] This may better be understood by comparing this early manifestation of intense feeling with that of a painting of the high Baroque, Rubens' 'Martyrdom of Saint Livinus' (Fig. 3). Rubens did not shrink from portraying the goriest details in his search for extreme emotional effects. As Saint Livinus looks up to heaven, the chief torturer displays a pair of tongs in which he holds the tongue that has just been torn from the saint's mouth.

4

Garnier, *Bradamante* (*c.* 1582)[1]

SUMMARY OF PLOT

Roger, a French knight, is shipwrecked on an island in the Mediterranean. Roland and some other knights find him there, approve his projected marriage with Bradamante, and then all set out for France. At the court, they find that Bradamante's parents are negotiating to marry her to Léon, son of the emperor of Greece. Roger becomes angry at Léon, disguises himself, and sets out to find him. He is captured at Novengrade and is rescued from death by Léon himself, who does not know who he is. Soon after this, Léon hears that Bradamante has decreed that anyone who wants to marry her must defeat her in battle. Léon asks Roger, who is still incognito, to win her for him and Roger feels obliged to give his consent. They go to the French court and Roger defeats Bradamante. Léon discovers Roger's identity and yields up his claim on Bradamante. The Bulgars send ambassadors to ask Roger to be their king and Bradamante's parents consent to their marriage.

PLOT SCHEME

Roger-Bradamante-Léon		French Nationalism and Christianity
	Act I	
		i
ii		ii
	Act II	
i		
ii		
iii		

Roger-Bradamante-Léon		French Nationalism and Christianity
	Act III	
i		
ii		
iii		
iv		
v		
vi		
	Act IV	
i		
ii		
iii		
iv		
v		v
vi		vi
	Act V	
i		
ii		ii
iii		
iv		iv
v		
		vi
vii		vii

PLOT

The plot of Garnier's *Bradamante* represents in the present study the first unequivocal departure from the traditional Renaissance mode. As is to be expected, however, this new manner of dealing with plot takes the form of another modest step away from the older method toward a different concept of dramatic action, rather than any radical upsetting of tradition. The action is generally dominated by the theme of Roger-Bradamante-Léon, but, at the same time, a new concept has entered in the form of a number of scenes that stand apart from this leading motive. It is significant of a new approach to the problem of dramatic action that the first act is devoted to matters not directly and necessarily connected with what is later to become the principal motive. The participation of the plot of Roger-Bradamante-Léon in I, ii is reduced to a mere mention of Roger and Bradamante in two lines. The brief first act, therefore, goes by without suggesting the course the action will follow. The will to an early variety of the displacement of the axis—i.e., the shifting of emphasis away from an element of greater to one of lesser importance—is evident.[2] The sharp contrast of this procedure with the techniques used in such plays as *Electra*, *Didon*, and *Hippolyte* hardly needs to be mentioned.

Acts II and III deal exclusively with the primary theme. Every scene of Act IV is built around the principals, although scenes v and vi include references to the ideological theme of French nationalism and Christianity. Act V is a curious sort of hybrid. The motive of nationalism and Christianity grows to an even larger importance, although it appropriates to itself exclusively only scene vi. The rest of the act is dominated by the plot of Roger-Bradamante-Léon, with the patriotic-religious theme serving as a running ideological accompaniment to the story of the fortunes of Roger and Bradamante, who are evidently intended to serve as the ideal embodiment of the national and religious virtues that are extolled.

Because of the preponderance of the principal motive, there is slight opportunity for the restless movement of plot elements that will be characteristic of the seventeenth-century theater. The only signs of a growing Baroque attitude toward plot are visible in the introduction of the prominent secondary theme of Christian nationalism. The amorphous masses of the typical seventeenth-century plot are in the present play in an early stage, although their development has unmistakably begun. As an example of the uncertainty regarding the denouement and the consequent restless movement of plot elements in their mutual relations, it will be sufficient to call attention to a few salient instances.

Act III ends with Bradamante's statement of her determination to kill the supposed Léon in their joust. This leaves the outcome of the

play highly uncertain and makes the course of the plot doubtful. This
fluid state of affairs lasts only until the first scene of Act IV, when it is
indicated that Bradamante has been defeated. As Léon is taking credit
for the victory, however, this creates an even worse difficulty, since the
desired issue is the marriage of Roger and Bradamante. In another
instance, the pause before the disclosure of Hippalque's plan for stop-
ping Bradamante's marriage works also to create, for a moment, an
atmosphere of uncertainty. And as late as V, ii, a new plot element is
introduced in the offer to Roger of the kingship of Bulgaria. This is a
key event and not simply a pleasant excess of frosting on the cake.

It is hardly necessary to point out that the Renaissance could not have
conceived of this practice as a possibility in a serious play. There is an
evident intent to mystify the audience at each new stage of plot development, although this tendency has not proceeded nearly so far as will be
the case during the seventeenth century. At the same time, it must be
pointed out that the viewpoint that governs the convolutions of the
plot in the work under consideration are equally far removed from
those of a generation or two before. *Bradamante* stands somewhere
between the Renaissance and the Baroque, and has fused the traditional
procedures with a number of innovations to form an artistic ideal that
belongs entirely to neither of these two esthetic movements. Or, to
state the circumstances with more precision, it subscribes whole-
heartedly to the esthetic of the last quarter of the sixteenth century and
did not pause to consider that it formed a part of an intermediate era
between two epochs of art history that would later be named Renaissance and Baroque.

The manner of treating the denouement is indicative of the position
of this play between the two artistic periods in question. Instead of concentrating the final resolution into a scene or two, as the seventeenth
century will do, Garnier spreads it out over the entire last act. First he
solves the problem by having Léon renounce Bradamante (V, i), then
he informs the court and Bradamante's parents (V, iv), and finally he
allows Hippalque to tell Bradamante of the happy solution (V, v). The
denouement still proceeds with the majestic, unhurried gait of a

Renaissance work. The ending anticipates the Baroque in that it has a strong element of surprise, but it leans toward the Renaissance in the early revelation of this surprise and in the slow pace of the last act.

The next to the last scene (V, vi), a soliloquy on Christian patriotism by a person who appears on stage only this one time, has a peculiar flavor that is neither Renaissance nor Baroque. The story, in full tilt toward the final scene of Roger's glorification, is suddenly suspended. Into this very prominent place, where under either Baroque or Renaissance standards one would expect to find a scene highly relevant to the stream of action, the author drops a quiet soliloquy on the ideological theme. The contrast between action and mere talk is strong and operates as a disturbing element that slows and obscures the progress of the story. In order to achieve full understanding of the differences in technique, it is expedient to recall that under the Baroque concept of art in the theater, there would by this time have occurred a complete fusion of themes. Hence, the feeling would have been one of constant acceleration of tempo and heightening of emotion until the brilliant conclusion. The hesitation before the finale is again indicative of an intermediate status in which both artistic ideals are compounded into a blend that is neither Renaissance nor Baroque but which belongs rather to an intermediate attitude. In the management of the plot, the Renaissance mode is still powerful in the tendency to make the central motive dominant at all points. At the same time, the Baroque procedure shows considerable strength in the presence of a sub-theme and in the trend toward a partial unclearness in the course of the action.

The characteristic mode of organizing time in *Bradamante* is not that of the Renaissance. That is to say, the scenes are not organized in succession along a single line of plot, nor do they proceed without distractions to a clearly anticipated ending. Neither can they be said to form, in the Baroque fashion, a number of plots that maintain a carefully separate existence in the early stages of the play but which steadily merge with each other as if they were pointed toward a single plot-idea complex that is revealed with dazzling effect at the end. After this exclusion of the work from an undivided participation in the technique of either one of the two periods by telling what it is not, it is necessary to describe carefully what it is.

As the preceding examination would lead one to deduce, the manner of handling the plot involves a thorough blending of the two styles, so that the technique is neither wholly Renaissance nor Baroque, but is rather a combination of these two modes of creating dramatic beauty, for which combination no traditional name exists in the history of literature.[3] The first act, which consists of only two scenes, revolves principally about the theme of Christian nationalism. Since the most important motif, that of the difficulties of Roger, Bradamante, and Léon, is barely mentioned, the situation here is similar to that in Lope's *Fuenteovejuna* (1619), in which the principal ideological theme and the chief plot-motive have no apparent connection with each other until toward the end of the last act. With Act II, however, this 'Baroque' plot situation comes to an abrupt end and the principal subject of the play remains dominant until the end. In spite of this, there is a considerable feeling for mystery in the process of complicating and finally unraveling the plot. It is not until II, i that the difficulties concerning Bradamante's marriage are referred to. Even here, the approach is slow and indirect. The opening lines of this scene serve rather to arouse curiosity than to satisfy it (pp. 319–20):

> Aymon
> Le party me plaist fort.
>   Béatrix
>   Aussi fait-il à moy.
>   Aymon
> J'en suis tout transporté.
>   Béatrix
>   Si suis-je, par ma foy.

After this exchange, the author is still not ready to introduce the leading motive. For a number of lines, Aymon and Béatrix lament the evil state into which the younger generation has fallen. Then, in a roundabout way, Garnier finally brings in the most important line of action as follows (p. 321):

> Aymon
> Léon le représente,
> Qui pour la seule amour recherche Bradamante.
>
> . . . .
>
> Béatrix
> Il est vray: mais pourtant ne sçavez-vous pas bien
> Que Roger est son âme, et sa vie et son bien?

After this oblique introduction to the story, the succeeding parts of the play keep it in a prominent place as the action unfolds. The fact that the principal subject remains obvious does not, however, militate against the presence of a constantly recurring uncertainty concerning the outcome. Act III ends with a soliloquy by Bradamante in which she vows to kill the supposed Léon. The audience must be aware that Roger will not be killed, but the problematical nature of the means to be used in keeping him safe constitutes a deviation from the earlier practice of a maximum certainty in the development of the plot. A further unclearness appears in IV, iii (p. 363). Hippalque attempts to console Bradamante by telling her that God can, if he so chooses, rescue her from this unhappy situation. Bradamante replies:

> Et comment? quel moyen? qu'à Léon j'obéisse
> Par ses armes vaincue, et sois impératrice?
> Ha! non! plustost la mort se coule dans mon sein . . .

The effect of these lines is to point up sharply the continuing problem of how the play will turn out. This problem assumes the form of a mysterious question whose answer will be difficult to find. Two solutions to the difficulty are offered—death or marriage to Léon—neither of which suggests what eventually happens.

One of the standard seventeenth-century devices for avoiding a clear and open exposition of the plot will be that of delay of an imminent

revelation. In IV, iv (pp. 366–67), this typical Baroque recourse occurs
in a mild form, that is, the delay is brief and creates less tension than will
be the case during the period that follows. Hippalque makes a suggestion that stirs up some excitement:

Hippalque
Je sçay bien un moyen pour brouiller tout l'affaire.
Marphise
Et quel? ma grand amie.
Bradamante
Et que faudrait-il faire?
Marphise
Je volle toute d'aise.
Bradamante
Hippalque, mon amour.
Marphise
Mon coeuret, je te pry, fay nous quelque bon tour.
Hippalque
La fourbe est bien aisée. Il faut que vous, Marphise,
. . . .
Soutenez qu'on fait tort à vostre frère absent,
Mariant Bradamante et la luy ravissant . . .

The remarks of Bradamante and Marphise, which are not necessary
to the unfolding of this scene, nevertheless have an indispensable function in the peculiar esthetic organization of parts, which is to delay the
revelation of Hippalque's plan and thereby create in the audience a
strong emotion whose core is furnished by a suddenly manufactured
tension. A further instance of the feeling aroused by mystery and uncertainty is afforded by the last act. The play is virtually over by V, i, but
interest remains at a high level because the exciting scene of Bradamante's discovery of Roger's presence is still to come. Coincident with
all the deviations from the straight path of logical development of the
story, there exists a strong affinity for a clear exposition of the dominant plot. These habits of artistic creation, if expressed in the terms of
the opposite poles of Baroque and Renaissance, may be described as a

liking for inevitability diffused through the play versus a feeling for mystery. As has been pointed out in other connections, *Bradamante* appears to be governed by neither of these opposed ideals in its pure form but rather to aim at some esthetic ground between the two. The migration, conscious or unconscious, toward a new mode of plot management is illustrated in a speech by Mélisse in V, vi (p. 395):

> Lors qu'on n'y pense point, son pouvoir il découvre:
> En faits désespérez miraculeux il ouvre.

These lines may be regarded as the embodiment of the newly arisen theories on how a plot should be handled. The entire scene in which these verses occur demands comment as an expression of the new attitudes toward dramatic form. This scene, a monolog by Mélisse on the topic of Christian patriotism, turns aside from the leading motive in the last moments of the play for a brief dissertation on a topic not absolutely necessary to the story. Although this would be a notable anomaly in a Renaissance drama, it has a well-marked role here. This function becomes apparent only if the existence of an ideological theme has previously been recognized. Under these circumstances, this scene falls into its proper perspective as a glorification of Catholic France.

The interest in concealing the course of the action from one scene to the next can be observed in such features as the uncertainty concerning the issue of the battle between Bradamante and the disguised Roger, as well as in the outcome of the seemingly insoluble difficulties that prevent Roger's marriage to Bradamante. With the beginning of Act V, this latter complication is resolved when Léon abdicates his claim to Bradamante. With this, the chief difficulty in the way of the happy solution of the story is cleared away and the outcome of the story becomes evident, but Garnier is intent on retaining to the end a certain amount of mysteriousness. This he succeeds in doing by leaving still unsolved the problem of how Aymon and Béatrix are to be persuaded to consent to the marriage. This last stumbling-block is removed with the utmost ease by transforming Roger into a king. This leaves the whole court staring at him in joyful admiration in a final scene of glorification that is a foreshadowing of the way in which this technique will be carried to its furthest extreme in the dazzling final scenes of such Baroque works as *Fuenteovejuna, Las mocedades del Cid*, and *La vida es sueño*. To state it briefly, the plot of *Bradamante* is organized on the broad principle of scenes strung along a single line of plot that proceed to an ending that is suspected from early in the play (i.e., from Act II) but whose solution is concealed until late in the play (i.e., until V, i). The level of interest is then sustained during the final act by playing on the audience's curiosity regarding the manner in which this solution will be made. The fact that this procedure constitutes a hybrid technique for which no name has been invented need not militate against its accurate description as a pattern of literary phenomena, nor is it to be construed as a shortcoming of the present play.

The Renaissance habit of reducing the action to a minimum of elapsed time is in this play still operative. It must be pointed out, however, that the stringency of this regulation is mitigated somewhat, not by any leaning toward a radically free treatment of the time element but rather by a failure to emphasize a strict conformity with the principle of minimum time. This is done by ordering the events of the story in such a way that the length of time involved is not indicated. For example, the battle between Roger and Bradamante takes place off stage immediately after the end of Act III. When Act IV opens, an indeterminate period has elapsed that may be as short as an hour or as long as a day. Under the Renaissance ideal of beauty, it was taken for granted that the time element in the drama should be so densely packed that it would be obvious that the time had been reduced to the smallest scope consonant with the satisfactory rendition of the plot, as is the case with Baïf's *Electra*. In *Bradamante*, this concept of time has been much vitiated; the close organization of time has lapsed by default without being replaced by the attitudes that will have arisen on this point within a few years.

It may not be without a certain value to the understanding of the esthetic transformations of the eras involved to point out that the principle of minimum time seems to have arisen, flourished, and now, in the late sixteenth century, to be disappearing simultaneously with the use of traditional subjects. This theory, that these two elements of familiar plots and the shortest elapsed time were tied together, finds support in the consideration that the use of well-known stories made it possible to dispense with any information concerning previous events and to proceed to the nub of the story without delay. This reduction of the plot to its most critical moments would at the same time make it feasible to reduce the time of the play to a very brief duration. As the effects of esthetic fatigue caused the playwrights to tire of the traditional Renaissance solutions, however, they began to use themes from European history and from earlier European literatures; the present work, borrowed from Ariosto, offers a case in point. This employment of a less familiar subject matter created a need for a more elaborate exposition and consequently for more elapsed time. In this connection, it needs to be emphasized that the explanation of this point is phrased not in the positivistic terms of an external cause that produces an artistic effect but rather in the esthetic terms of an autonomous art form that is gradually transformed as the governing feeling for beauty changes. It is expedient to make a further precautionary remark to the effect that, in all that has been said, no implication is intended in regard to the extent to which the author may have been aware of the esthetic attitudes that his work embodies. Here, as elsewhere in the present study, the intention is in the main descriptive rather than speculative.

STYLE

In the configurations of the language, typical Renaissance figures of speech occur with moderate frequency. In III, ii (p. 349), Bradamante apostrophizes Roger in these terms:

> Las! votre seule absence est cause de ma plainte!
> Comme, quand le soleil cache au soir sa clairté,
> Vient la palle frayeur avec l'obscurité,
> Mais si tost qu'apparoist sa rayonnante face,

> La nuit sombre nous laisse, et la crainte se passe;
> Ainsi sans mon Roger je suis toujours en peur . . .

The simile here is easily recognizable because it is founded on a physical contrast that is universally familiar as well as because the mode of
its statement is direct and brief. It is, in short, quite in keeping with the
traditions of the Renaissance. Another figure of much the same nature
occurs a few lines below:

> Comme durant l'hyver, quand le soleil s'absente
> Que nos jours sont plus courts, sa torche moins ardente,
> Viennent les Aquilons dans le ciel tempester,
> On voit sur les rochers les neiges s'afester,
> Les glaces et frimas rendre la terre dure,
> Le bois rester sans feuille et le pré sans verdure:
> Ainsi quand vous, Roger, vous absentez de moy,
> Je suis en un hyver de tristesse et d'esmoy.

This comparison, like the one that has just been remarked upon, is
conventional and is stated directly, without the accumulation of a large
number of tropes and without the deliberate shock of the bizarre conceit that is so common in the high Baroque. The obvious, formal
scaffolding of 'Comme . . . Ainsi . . .' is also typical of the sixteenth-
century rendering of the figure of speech. This same structural peculiarity lends its rigid support to a comparison of Roger with a tower in
his firm resistance to Bradamante's attacks, in IV, i (p. 358):

> Comme une forte tour sur le rivage assise,
> Par les vagues battue et par la froide bise,
> Ne s'en esbranle point, dure contre l'effort
> De l'orage qui bruit et tempeste si fort,
> Ainsi luy sans ployer sous l'ardente furie
> Et les aspres assauts de sa douce ennemie . . .

A further simile of this kind occurs in this same speech (p. 359), with
the familiar 'comme . . . ainsi.'

G

> Comme un qui pour forcer une ville travaille,
> Ceinte de grands fossez et d'épaisse muraille
>
> . . . .
>
> La vierge ainsi se peine, et tant moins elle espère
> Vaincre son ennemi, d'autant plus se colère . . .

Aside from these vestiges of an earlier attitude toward style, the forms and spirit seem to look largely toward the Baroque. In I, i (especially p. 314), the extravagant tone of Charlemagne's praise of his knights denotes a new feeling. He says (p. 314):

> Ils ont domté l'Asie et l'Afrique, courans
> De rivage en rivage, ainsi que gros torrens
> Qui tombent en avril des négeuses montagnes,
> Et passent en bruyant à travers les campagnes,
> Rompent tout, faucent tout, arrachent les ormeaux,
> Entraînent les bergers, leurs cases et troupeaux.

The almost chaotic haste with which the verbs follow each other and the impetuous speed with which the metaphor is developed belong to a new way of looking at the rendition of dramatic dialog and are remote from the majestic, unhurried dignity of a generation before.[4] A few lines farther on (p. 315), Charlemagne refers in bizarre, extravagant figures of speech to the large numbers of the Moors:

> Ils couvroyent de leurs rangs la poudroyante plaine.
> Leurs chevaux espuisoyent les claires eaux de Seine.
> L'air résonnait de cris, les bataillons pressez
> Mouvoyent de toutes parts de picques herissez.

The same tendency toward heaping up exaggerated metaphors appears in Bradamante's description of her loneliness since Roger has been away. In III, ii (p. 348), she says:

> Comme un rocher privé de ses roses vermeilles,
> Un pré de sa verdure, un taillis de ses feuilles,

> Un ruisseau de son onde, un champ de ses épis,
> Telle je suis sans vous, telle et encore pis.

The Baroque fondness for contrast is in evidence in this play, although it is not exploited to the extent that will later be the case. In IV, ii (p. 361), Roger wishes for death after his victory over Bradamante: 'O terre, ouvre ton sein! ô ciel, lasche ton foudre . . .' It is typical of an incipient Baroque approach to artistic expression that the metaphor here is cast in terms of the sharp opposition of earth and sky. The same feeling for contrast furnishes the (probably unconscious) motivation for the opposition between Bradamante's emotions immediately before and after Hippalque tells her that Roger is at court and is to marry her. Her sadness in the first part of this scene (V, v) stands out sharply against her joy when she is finally convinced that Hippalque is telling the truth.

One of the most noticeable distinctions between the respective approaches to the theater on the part of the sixteenth and seventeenth centuries resides in the extensive exploitation of humor in the latter as against its almost complete absence in the serious plays of the former. The Renaissance, in its consistent devotion to a monumental dignity in the serious drama, did not conceive of the possibility of levity in such a work. The Baroque, on the other hand, discarded this decorous view of dramatic action in favor of a wider emotional spectrum capable of including the expression, within a single play, of such widely disparate attitudes as the most abandoned sorrow and the slapstick humor of low comedy. In the work now under investigation, the use of humor is slight when it is compared with the Spanish *comedia* of the seventeenth century, although it does represent some increase over that of Garnier's own *Hippolyte* of nine years before. This, like some of its other qualities, is indicative of the intermediate status of the esthetics of the late sixteenth century. The expression of the comical in *Bradamante* is, as would be expected on theoretical grounds, more restrained than is the case with the Baroque. In II, iii (p. 340), Béatrix ridicules Bradamante's insistence that her suitors must fight her:

> Qui jamais ouït dire
> Que pour se marier il se fallust occire?
> Les combats de l'amour ne sont guères sanglans;
> Ils se font en champs clos entre des linceulx blancs,
> On y est désarmé: car d'Hymen les querelles
> Se vuident seulement par armes naturelles.

In II, ii (p. 333), there occurs the device, so familiar to students of the *comedia*, of putting a comical remark in the mouth of a servant. Aymon, who has flown into a rage at Renaud's opposition to Bradamante's projected marriage to Léon, promises to do great carnage among those who dare to go against his will. La Roque then says:

> Ils ru'ra de beaux coups:
> Dieu me veuille garder s'il m'atteint d'avanture.

In II, i (p. 320), Aymon makes a remark that reveals his sly self-interest:

> Ce que je prise plus en si belle alliance,
> C'est qu'il ne faudra point desbourser de finance.
> Il ne demande rien.

The general emotional atmosphere of *Bradamante* has moved far afield from that of the plays of a generation or two before. In the present case, the tone has gravitated toward the Baroque ideal of strong emotion of an intimately personal character and away from the serene imperturbability of the Renaissance theater. This highly personal mood is established in the first scene by Charlemagne's frequent references to himself and is sustained throughout the play. The attitudes of the Renaissance in these matters have fallen completely into desuetude. The quarrel of Aymon and Renaud over Bradamante's marriage (II, ii) conforms to this new feeling. This disagreement between father and son is domestic in nature and involves the representation of tempestuous feelings that are highly individualized. Even more thoroughly domestic is the following scene (II, iii), in which Béatrix attempts to advise Bradamante concerning the choice of a husband; the whole scene partakes of the nature of a crisis that transpires in the bosom of the family.

In III, i (p. 345), Roger shows a weakness and trembling before his thoughts of love that are characteristic of this new position in regard to emotion. He says:

> Ma force s'affoiblist; frissoner je me voy;
> Mon sang et sens se trouble et ne suis plus à moy.

There is a visible contrast of the attitudes that govern this speech with those of Orestes in Baïf's *Electra*, who would have been incapable of expressing any of his sentiments in these soft, melancholy, non-heroic terms. The same sharp distinction with the Renaissance mode of delineating strong feeling is evident in Roger's soliloquy in III, v, where, disguised as Léon, he is prepared to do battle with Bradamante. The tone is one of sad complaint and hopeless rebellion, and bears no resemblance to the unyielding stoicism of the Renaissance hero. The atmosphere of non-heroic family relationships is strictly preserved in Aymon's apology to Roger when he accepts him as Bradamante's husband (V, iv). He says (p. 388):

> Roger, mon cher enfant, ça, que je vous embrasse.
> J'ay grand-peur que je sois en votre male-grâce:
> Pardonnez-moy, mon fils, si j'ay si longuement
> Tenu par mi rigeur vos amours en tourment.

Garnier's attitude toward these emotional effects is concisely stated in a speech by Hippalque in V, v. In an almost hysterical excess of joy over the discovery of Roger's true identity, she says (p. 390):

> Je ne sçay que je fais, tant je suis hors de moy:
> Qui eust jamais pensé d'une amère tristesse
> Voir sourdre tout soudain une telle liesse?

Garnier carefully stresses the joy that Bradamante will feel at the good news, as well as emphasizing her present sadness. This deliberately prepares the audience for the revelation, so that the emotional impact of the contrast of joy and sorrow may be observed closely and enjoyed to the full. It should be pointed out, however, that this exploitation of feeling has not yet (that is, by 1582) been pushed to the extreme limits that it will attain during the seventeenth century in such works of the plastic arts as the statue of Santa Teresa by Bernini and such typical examples of the *comedia* as Lope's *Fuenteovejuna*.[5]

The love of heightened emotion finds expression also in the deliberately created tension that is so distinctive a feature of the Baroque drama and which is employed a number of times in *Bradamante*. In IV, iv, Hippalque tells Bradamante and Marphise that she has found a way to prevent Bradamante's marriage to Léon. They press her to tell them, which she soon does, but their excited requests themselves, which are not strictly necessary to the development of the action, function to delay Hippalque's disclosure of her plan. This acts to raise emotion to a high pitch in the audience, since they are eager to see if the new idea is feasible. At the same time, the delay is brief, unlike the elaborate and long-sustained moments of uncertainty in the Baroque theater proper.

A similar situation of manufactured suspense occurs in V, iv, where Roger's identity is at last revealed to the court. Léon and Roger alone know who it is that fought Bradamante. The audience knows that Roger must be discovered in this scene and has ample opportunity to enjoy it as the moment of disclosure approaches. Aymon expresses concisely the question that is torturing the curiosity of the members of the court (p. 385): 'Qui est cet abuseur? d'où nous est-il venu?' This question, whose answer is already known to the audience, serves to organize, focus, and raise to an even higher pitch the feelings that cluster around the mystery of the masked man.

The solution of the plot-problem has become clear by V, i, when it is apparent that Léon will relinquish Bradamante to Roger. In order to sustain interest, the author, who can no longer make use of mystery concerning the denouement, has recourse to the creation of emotional tension. That is, he fails to inform Bradamante of the course of events, so that he still has to show the exciting and emotionally satisfying scene of her discovery that she is to marry Roger, as well as the hero's glorification by the Bulgarian ambassadors and the French court.

The paradox is exploited in the work under examination with something approaching the consistency and frequency of the high Baroque theater. The whole situation of the play is contradictory in nature; that is, Léon wants Bradamante but cannot win her himself, so he asks his friend to help him. Roger himself is in love with Bradamante but feels constrained to keep silent and comply with Léon's request. This inevitably leads to a situation in which Roger wins Bradamante but has to give her to Léon. The extreme difference between this mode of handling action and the direct exposition of the Renaissance play is apparent enough. Garnier, determined to be fully understood and to secure the participation of the audience in the esthetic effects that he is seeking, makes a carefully concise statement of this contradiction. In III, i (p. 347), Roger says:

> Il me fault despouiller moymesme de mon bien,
> Délivrer à un autre un amour qui est mien,
> En douer mon contraire, et l'emplir de liesse,
> M'enfiellant l'estomach d'une amère tristesse.

In order that the present discussion of the appearance of an early Baroque technique should not be misconstrued, it is necessary to observe that there are conflicting motives in Renaissance drama as well. The distinction to be made here is that in the Renaissance these conflicting motives are not stated in such a way as to give them the air of mutually contradictory opposites, whereas the Baroque technique deliberately creates and dwells on the paradox. In III, v (p. 353), Roger again states the opposed circumstances and does so in a series of parallel forms that call attention to the contradictions contained in them. He says:

> Me voici déguisé, mais c'est pour me tromper.
> Je porte un coutelas, mais c'est pour m'en frapper.

> J'entre dans le combat pour me vaincre moymesme.
> Le prix de ma victoire est ma dépouille mesme.

Here, the conflicting circumstances are stated four times in as many lines. Here and elsewhere, the author patently savors the contradiction and expects that the audience shall do the same. In IV, iii (p. 362), Bradamante says, 'Las! Roger, où es-tu? où es-tu ma chère âme?' Here, the paradox depends on the audience's knowledge that Roger is nearby in the person of the pseudo-Léon but that Bradamante herself does not suspect it. The same attitudes govern Bradamante's expression of sorrow because she thinks that Roger does not know of her published intention to duel with any prospective suitor. She says (p. 363):

> Chacun l'a sceu, Roger: les peuples ibérides,
> Les Mores, les Persans, les Gètes, les Colchides,
> Et tu l'ignores seul: cela toy seul ne sçais
> Qu'espandre pour toy seul par le monde je fais.

The intimate atmosphere of *Bradamante* affects the nature of the ideology, which, by including frequent references to contemporary questions, encourages the spectator to participate actively in the work of art. These ideas are made to cluster about two prominent concepts that seem to present themselves to the author as a single complex made up of Christianity and French nationalism. This is in direct opposition to the Renaissance practice of ignoring matters of mere contemporary interest, perhaps because of the insistence on generality during this period. The references to Christianity and nationalism usually accompany each other in *Bradamante* and are frequent and direct. The opening scene, a monolog by Charlemagne, is a glorification of God and France. The first line of the play (p. 313) epitomizes this scene, when Charlemagne says, 'Les sceptres des grands rois viennent du Dieu suprême.'

In III, v (p. 353), Roger says, 'Qui suis-je? où suis-je? où vay-je? O dure destinée!' These questions not only betray the intense interest that is growing up in the theater concerning the individual and his personality, but involves as well a bitter questioning of fate and a doubt regarding man's ultimate destination that are part of the Baroque manner of looking at life.[6] The man of the Renaissance, with his tranquil assurance of the excellence of this life and its fulness of meaning and of the security of the life to come, would have been less inclined to ask this question.

Religion and nationalism are linked together in V, v, in a bloodthirsty monolog spoken by Mélisse. Much the same spirit lies behind Bradamante's soliloquy in III, vi; Léon's speech to Charlemagne in IV, v (pp. 367–68); and the long speech by the Bulgarian ambassadors in V, ii (pp. 380–82). It is evident that by 1582 the international spirit of Catholicism has been transformed into one of national pride. This national-Christian ideology is perfectly fused into the plot that revolves about Roger and Bradamante, so that it is focused on and expressed through their persons and finds issue in the optimistic atmosphere of the last act. This cheerful spirit is epitomized in the two concluding lines (p. 397) spoken by Léon:

O! que je suis heureux! Je vaincray désormais
L'heur des mieux fortunez qui vesquirent jamais.

The happy ending, which will become standard in the Spanish *comedia*, corresponds to the desperate and aggressive insistence on optimism that represents a strong reaction against the doubts that were beginning to appear, to the effect that all might not be right with the world, that God might be a myth, and that the dogma of an anthropocentric religion might be a pious and wishful fraud.

A common recourse of the new feeling for style is the statement of opposed ideas in parallel structural forms, whose occurrence in earlier plays has already been pointed out in the present study. This device is used with moderate frequency in the present play and holds close to the Baroque patterns that have been described. In II, i, Aymon and Béatrix are discussing Bradamante's marriage. In an alternation of speeches of one line each, they express their divergent ideas (pp. 323–24):

Béatrix

Si ne devons-nous pas contraindre son désir.

Aymon

Si ne doit-elle pas en faire à son plaisir.

Béatrix

La voudriez-vous forcer en un si libre affaire?

Aymon

Elle doit approuver ce qui plaist à son père.

Béatrix

L'amour ne se gouverne à l'appétit d'autruy.

Aymon

L'on ne peut gouverner les enfans d'aujourdhuy.

Béatrix

S'il n'y a de l'amour, ils n'auront point de joye.

Aymon

L'amour sous le devoir des mariages ploye.

Béatrix

Rien n'y est si requis que leur consentement.

Aymon

Rien n'y est si requis que mon consentement.

If this passage is compared with the similar ones in Baïf's *Electra*, which are discussed above, it is evident that Garnier exploits parallelism of form and opposition of meaning much more deliberately than does Baïf.

In III, i (p. 348), Roger refers to his paradoxical relation to Léon in opposed half-lines:

Celuy que j'offensois à mon bien se trouva.
Je le cherchais à mort, il me donna la vie.
J'estois jaloux de luy, je luy livre m'amie.

In III, i (p. 345), Léon innocently remarks to Roger that, since he did the fighting, he is the one entitled to marry Bradamante. He says, 'Las! frère, c'est de vous qu'elle deust estre dame.' Roger and the audience know of his love for Bradamante but Léon, who makes this comment with its unwitting *double entendre*, does not. Léon's meaning is in

contrast to the additional significance that it contains for Roger; this opposition increases the impact of the double meaning and functions to raise
emotion to a higher pitch than would have been possible without the
use of this irony of circumstance expressed in a paradox. In I, ii (p. 317),
paired single lines are followed by two groups of three lines each:

> Charlemagne
> Nous contenterons-nous de les vaincre à demy?
> Nymes
> Ne vous suffist-il pas de chasser l'ennemy?
> Charlemagne
> Ce ne m'est pas assez de défendre ma terre.
> Nymes
> Que demandez-vous plus que d'achever la guerre?
> Charlemagne
> Un empereur romain ne se peut dire avoir
> Pour chasser un Barbare assez fait de devoir
> Qui pourra retourner avec nouvelle force.
> Nymes
> Son malheureux succez ne luy sert pas d'amorce
> Pour franchir de rechef les rochers Pyrénez,
> Et repiller encor nos champs abandonnez.

In II, ii (p. 331), Aymon and Renaud dispute bitterly over Bradamante's marriage:

> Aymon
> Un enfant doit tousjours obéir à son père.
> Renaud
> S'il va de son dommage il ne le doit pas faire.
> Aymon
> Sur ses enfans un père ha toute authorité.
> Renaud
> Quand leur bien il procure et leur utilité.
> Aymon
> Est-il père si dur qui leur perte pourchasse?
> Renaud
> Je croy qu'il n'en est point qui sciemment le face.

In every case, two characters who are in disagreement state their respective arguments in passages that are noticeably similar in form and dissimilar in thought. This use of contrast embedded in parallel forms is found also in III, v (p. 354), where Roger says:

> A mon sort les Enfers de semblable n'ont rien:
> Ils ont divers tourmens, mais moy je suis le mien,
> Moymesme me punis, moymesme me bourrelle;
> Je suis mon punisseur et ma peine cruelle;
> Je me suis ma Mégère et mes noirs coulevreaux,
> Mes cordes et mes fers, mes fouets et mes flambeaux.

The paradox in these instances lies in the fact that a man should execute his own punishment, as Roger feels that he is doing. In addition to these contrastive ideas, there is a peculiarly Baroque coloration to be seen in the marked consciousness of one's own feelings and the extravagant fashion in which they are expressed.

A further point to be made concerning the gradual shift to a new esthetic mode is the appearance of the practice of playing on words. In V, v (p. 392), Hippalque assures Bradamante that Roger is really at the court: 'Non, ce que je vous dy n'est songe ne mensonge.' This juggling of words that are similar in sound is still conservative but it marks a radical departure from the Renaissance style in serious plays, in which puns and jokes were virtually unknown. The appearance of this characteristic device is significant of a budding predilection for decorative passages that correspond to the liking for surface decoration that will become such a prominent feature in the drama, sculpture, and architecture of the seventeenth century.

CHARACTERS

The characters are managed in such a way that they too take part in the mildly restless movement characteristic of the early Baroque drama. This finds expression in the failure of the principals to follow unswervingly the course of action to which they have apparently been bound. In III, i (p. 347), Roger's appeal to the stars to let him die diverges from the attitudes of the preceding period in its helpless resignation. The Renaissance hero or heroine never wavers and never despairs. In Baïf's play, Electra pursues a given course of action without thought of deviating from it for any reason. To his feeling of despair, Roger adds an uncertainty that was unknown to the hero of the earlier sixteenth-century theater. In III, i (p. 348), he says:

> Las! je ne sçay; je suis
> En une mer de maux, en un gouffre d'ennuis.

After a fashion that will during the next century petrify into an accepted artistic convention, Roger is pulled simultaneously toward two opposite courses of conduct. In III, v, he argues with himself over the question of keeping the promise made to Léon to do battle with Bradamante or to refuse to do so and thereby be dishonored. He says (p. 354):

> Encor si à moy seul je faisois cet outrage.
> Mais Bradamante, hélas! le souffre davantage.
> Il faut n'en faire rien. Mais quoy! tu l'as promis.
> C'est tout un; ne m'en chaut: il n'estoit pas permis.
> Si ma promesse estoit de faire à Dieu la guerre,
> A mon père, à ma race, à ma natale terre,
> La devroy-je tenir? non, non, serait mal fait.
> De promesse méchante est très méchant l'effet.
> Voire, mais tu luy es attenu de ta vie.

These changes in emotional attitudes are quite similar to, though much less marked than, the fluctuation of Ximena between love and duty in both Corneille's *Le Cid* (1637) and Guillen de Castro's *Las mocedades del Cid* (1618).[7]

The personality of Bradamante, like that of Roger, was created under the guiding influence of a new feeling for dramatic beauty and no longer has the imperturbable quality of the Renaissance theater. In II, iii, her mother (Béatrix) is talking to Bradamante of her good fortune in having received a proposal of marriage from Léon. Bradamante says (p. 335):

> Las! Madame, je n'ay d'autre bonheur envie
> Que d'estre avecque vous tout le temps de ma vie.

For Garnier, the ideal heroine is no longer rigidly devoted to a single course of action, but has become soft and feminine, subject to bewilderment and driven by external forces which she cannot begin to control and which she understands imperfectly if at all. In short, Bradamante's assigned personality has gravitated far along the path toward a Baroque attitude toward personality.

In III, i (p. 344), Rogers says, 'Ah, quel malheur me suit! méchante destinée!' with a tender sentiment of melancholy that is unknown to the serious theater of the preceding generation. In this same scene (p. 348), Roger cannot decide what he should do to keep from losing Bradamante. He says, 'Hélas! non. Mais quoy donc? Las! je ne sçay...' The Renaissance hero is a stranger to this confusion, nor would he be likely to express his love in such soft, non-heroic terms as those used by Roger here and elsewhere in this scene (p. 345). He says, 'Ma force s'affoiblist; frissonner je me voy...' In Roger's monolog in III, v, the tone is melancholy and complaining in contradistinction to the heroic stoicism of an earlier period. Passages of this same nature spoken by Bradamante and Léon are so plentiful that their documentation can be dispensed with. This play, therefore, individualizes its personages more than is the case with previous works, and personality tends toward a certain emotional softness and lack of assurance, a wavering in choosing the course that is to be taken. This militates to a certain degree against the absolute clarity of the Renaissance but does not go as far in this respect as will the high Baroque.

A certain lack of consistency in the depiction of two of the minor characters may be remarked upon here. In II, i (p. 324), Béatrix insists that her daughter must marry a man she loves, which means that she should marry Roger. Later (II, iii, pp. 334–43), she pushes Bradamante to accept Léon's offer. In the latter part of this scene, Bradamante's threat to enter a convent frightens her mother so much that the latter insists fervently that Roger is the only one she should consider marrying. By IV, v (p. 371), Béatrix has forgotten all this and is enraged at Marphise's suggestion that Bradamante is already promised to Roger. Léon's activities and attitudes are characterized by the same absence of internal consistency and coherence. He first appears to be a conscienceless rogue so little given to introspection that he is unaware of his own unattractive nature. In IV, vi (p. 377), the imminent danger of the public exposure of his dishonesty in allowing Roger to fight for him brings home the fact of his unworthiness, but his only regret is that the French court will despise him. But in V, i (pp. 378ff), he is the soul of gentlemanly behaviour in his generous renunciation of his claims on Bradamante. These inconsistencies in the conduct of Béatrix and Léon are all the more noticeable because of the unity and coherence that characterize the deportment of the rascally Aymon, as well as that on the part of the two principals. This failure to achieve consistency of personality in a pair of minor characters is not to be regarded as a general artistic objective of either the Renaissance or the Baroque nor of the intermediate period under consideration, but is rather to be thought of tentatively as a trait that springs from an unthinking adherence to the details of Ariosto's poem. It goes without saying that it is not necessarily to be regarded as an artistic virtue.

It is significant of a new feeling toward the characters that there are several scenes in which only lesser personages are on the stage. If Léon is counted as a minor figure, there are eleven scenes out of a total of twenty-four that occur without the presence of either of the principals. That is, the secondary actors sometimes gravitate to the foreground and make a display of strictly personal qualities that have no necessary connection with the main line of the story nor to the leading characters. The case of Charlemagne in I, i and ii has been cited, and indeed in a number of other scenes he has more importance than would be given to any tributary person in a Renaissance play (e.g., see IV, v and V, iii and vii). A curious example appears in V, vi, where Mélisse engages in a monolog on Christian nationalism. Although she is so unessential to the action that she appears only this one time, her speech occupies a prominent position, since the next to the last scene of a play is second in importance only to the final scene itself. The use of a relatively insignificant personage as the mouthpiece of the ideology shows how the attitude toward tributary characters has changed.[8] In II, ii, Garnier delineates at some length the pettish bad temper and dishonesty of Aymon, convicting him through his own words of being a selfish, ambitious old man. It is hardly necessary to labor the point that this practice comes, not from any demand of the developing plot, but from a different concept of the way in which personality should be depicted. The incipient Baroque position in these matters is that human psychology is to be thought of in terms of a depth, complexity, and variety that did not occur to the dramatic authors of the Renaissance. This is not to be interpreted as an invidious distinction between the two periods, in which the Baroque comes off best. The only intent is to describe a characteristic difference in the mode of conceiving personality in the drama, not to imply the superiority of one style over the other. The quarrel between Aymon and Renaud over Bradamante's marriage offers a further illustration of the practice of depicting emotions in a highly individualized manner. It is also pertinent to this line of argument to recall Aymon's comical satisfaction over the fact that Léon has not asked for a dowry for Bradamante (p. 320, 'Ce que je prise plus . . .').

The existence of relationships between some of the minor actors in the drama also functions to distract attention from the leading characters and to make possible an attenuated version of absolute unity. The relationships between Aymon and Béatrix and between Renaud and Aymon furnish pertinent examples. The relation of minor personages to major has also undergone a radical transformation. Hippalque and La Roque, to take the humblest ones, no longer revolve exclusively around mistress and master. La Roque's mocking remark concerning Aymon's bloodthirsty threat is a case in point. A further instance of this tendency is found in Hippalque's confident intervention to suggest that Marphise stop the impending marriage by saying that Bradamante is already promised to Roger. Because of these new elements in their relations, the characters no longer seem mutually detached. The relationships are no longer impersonal and exclusive, and the body of characters tends to blur into a mass of figures tied together by a maze of personal connections. This situation contrasts with the earlier organization into two files of characters, each file dependent on one of the principals.

This investigation of the formal nature of *Bradamante* suggests a number of tentative conclusions. The old feeling for the conventional Renaissance tragedy has by this time been largely lost and has not yet been supplanted by a fully developed Baroque attitude, so that this play has the characteristics of both of these artistic commonwealths.[9]

It is not merely in the happy ending that this work differs from the usual tragedy of an earlier time. From beginning to end, it represents a further step in the steady drift toward a different conception of dramatic expression. This should not be read to signify that Garnier was struggling, with only partial success, to reach a higher and better vision of the dramatic art which would not be attained to the full until the time of Corneille and Racine. On the contrary, he, like all serious artists, gave an accurate expression of the concept of the beautiful that animated him and his contemporaries. It is only from the commanding vantage point afforded by a longer historical perspective that the critic of the twentieth century is able to perceive that *Bradamante* was simply a way station on the road of art, as are all specific works and all periods of art history. This is not to say that art is always becoming better but only that it is constantly in the process of changing into something different. The idea of amelioration in art is not admissible, although that of constant transformation is necessary to an understanding of the history of art.

Notes

¹ Garnier, *Oeuvres complètes*, II, 307–97. Subsequent references to *Bradamante* are to this edition. The lines are not numbered in this work.

² Rembrandt's 'Christ at Emmaus' (Fig. 8) illustrates the displacement of the axis in painting. Christ, who is obviously the chief figure, is placed to the left of the center of the picture. This displacement is emphasized by the fact that he is seated before an arched niche but is located a little to the left of its center-line. An examination of Raphael's 'School of Athens' (Fig. 9) makes apparent the contrasting practices of the Renaissance in respect to the organization of space. The two central figures are placed in the mechanical center of the composition. Their central position is strongly emphasized by a series of arches that have a common center-line. In the one case, every effort is made to assert the organizing value of the center by placing the chief element there. In the other, it is systematically denied.

³ If the literary critic should see fit to extend still further the borrowing of terminology from the plastic arts, it would be possible to adopt the designation 'Mannerism,' which historians of painting regularly use to denote that period of art history that falls between the Renaissance and the Baroque.

⁴ There is considerable formal similarity between this passage and the following one, taken from the seventeenth-century Spanish play *Las mocedades del Cid*, written in 1618 by Guillén de Castro. Here, the Moorish king surrenders to the Cid in Act II, ll. 1639ff:

> Tienes, Señor, un vasallo
> de quien lo son quatro reyes.
> En esquadrones formados,
> tendidas nuestras banderas,
> corríamos tus fronteras,
> vencíamos tus soldados,
> talávamos tus campañas,
> cautivávamos tus gentes,
> sugetando hasta las fuentes
> de las sobervias montañas;
> quando gallardo y ligero
> el gran Rodrigo llegó
> peleó, rompió, mató,
> y vencióme a mí el primero.

⁵ A detailed analysis of *Fuenteovejuna*, similar to those of the present study, is made in Darnell Roaten and F. Sánchez y Escribano, *Wölfflin's Principles in Spanish Drama: 1500–1700* (New York, 1952), pp. 96–132.

The forms of Bernini's 'Santa Teresa' (Fig. 7) are carefully disposed to exploit to the full the quasi-sexual voluptuousness that characterizes the scene that is depicted. The face and body of the saint express a complete abandonment to the spiritual experience which is described in her autobiography. The angel, who stands ready to pierce her heart with the mystic arrow, has a bodily grace and a coquettish smile that are highly sensual in nature. Even the restless, shifting folds of Santa Teresa's robe aid in suggesting an emotional turbulence that was foreign to the Renaissance mode of artistic expressiveness. The delineation of a spiritual event in terms that are charged with sexual feeling is characteristic of Baroque esthetics in both the theater and the plastic arts, while it is generally unknown to the Renaissance.

[6] For a brief analysis of a similar question in a high Baroque play, Guillén de Castro's *Las mocedades del Cid* (1618), see Roaten and Sánchez y Escribano, *Wölfflin's Principles*, p. 143, n. 2.

[7] For an analysis of *Le Cid*, see below. For an examination of *Las mocedades* similar to the present study, see Roaten and Sánchez y Escribano, *Wölfflin's Principles*, pp. 134ff.

[8] The location of a secondary figure in the place of greatest importance is frequently met with in Baroque painting. In Vermeer's 'Officer and Laughing Girl' (Fig. 2), attention is focused on the girl but the most prominent position in the picture-space is occupied by the officer. His seemingly paramount role is further enhanced by the fact that his red coat is the most brilliant spot of color in the picture. These formal distractions, however, are merely apparent. The forms are disposed in such a way that the spectator's eye is directed back to the principal figure along the strong diagonal that is established from the figure of the officer on one side to that of the girl on the other.

[9] Brueghel's 'Hunters in the Snow' (Fig. 10), like *Bradamante* and *Hippolyte*, exhibits the formal characteristics of both periods. The strong diagonal of the trees that extend into the picture from the left foreground is a mark of the new feeling for recession. This diagonal movement is reinforced by the houses on the left and by the movement of men and dogs along this line. The Renaissance predilection for plane organization is visible in the division of the frozen pond into discrete planes by means of a number of bands of buildings and snow that are in every case parallel to the picture frame. The Renaissance ideal of absolute clarity is expressed in the clear outlines of the trees already mentioned, as well as those of the figures of the men and dogs beneath them. The Baroque feeling makes its appearance in the relative indistinctness of the trees arranged along the foot of the hill in the foreground; here, the clear delineation of each branch is abandoned in favor of a relative unclearness that still does not interfere with the recognition of these objects as trees. The transition from the forms of the Renaissance to those of the Baroque is as evident in painting as in the theater.

5

Hardy, *La belle égyptienne* (c. 1615)[1]

SUMMARY OF PLOT

Don Jean de Carcame falls in love with Précieuse, a beautiful gypsy girl. He leaves home and joins her tribe in order to win her, taking the name of Andrès. Don Sancho does the same, taking the name of Clément. In a certain village, a girl named Carduche sees Andrès, falls in love with him, and proposes to him. He refuses and she puts into his bag one or two articles that belong to her. She accuses him of theft, his bag is searched, and the articles are found. A soldier becomes angry and slaps Andrès, who kills him on the spot. He is taken to jail and Précieuse appeals to Guiomar, the wife of the local alcalde, to save Andrès. The old gypsy woman confesses that she kidnapped Précieuse many years before and that she is the daughter of Ferdinand and Guiomar. Andrès is freed and Précieuse's parents consent to their marriage.

PLOT SCHEME

Andrès-Précieuse	Clément-Précieuse	Ferdinand-Guiomar-Précieuse	Carduche-Andrès
		Act I	
i (p. 111, l.1–p. 119, l.8)			
	ii (119, 9–119, 32)		
		Act II	
	i (120, 33–121, 64)		
ii (121, 65–122, 12)			

Andrès-Précieuse	Clément-Précieuse	Ferdinand-Guiomar-Précieuse	Carduche-Andrès
		iii (122, 13–124, 84)	
iv (124, 85–128, 40)			
		Act III	
	i (129, 41–130, 76)		
ii (130, 77–132, 41)	ii		
iii (132, 41–134, 100)			
iv (134, 1–135, 38)			
v	v (135, 39–137, 100)		
		Act IV	
			i (138, 1–138, 32)
ii	ii (139, 33–140, 92)		
			iii (140, 98–142, 62)
iv (142, 63–143, 6)			
			v (143, 7–144, 50)
vi (145, 51–145, 72)			
vii			vii (145, 73–148, 38)

Andrès-Précieuse	Clément-Précieuse	Ferdinand–Guiomar-Précieuse	Carduche-Andrès
		Act V	
		i (148, 39–149, 96)	
		ii (149, 97–151, 54)	
		iii (152, 55–152, 77)	
iv (152, 79–153, 10)			
		v (153, 11–157, 38)	
vi		vi (157, 39–159, 6)	

PLOT

A casual glance at the plot scheme will indicate the possibility of and need for a fusion of motives. The story consists of four distinct plots which must be joined in some way. In the early part of the play, the two motives of Andrès-Précieuse and of Clément-Précieuse carry the action alone. There is at first little or no visible connection between them, and it is only as the story develops that it is possible to see that the prime function of the theme of Clément-Précieuse is to make possible the convergence in time that is a part of the Baroque concept of dramatic beauty. Half way through Act II, the second major subject is introduced in the persons of Ferdinand and Guiomar. As is the case with Clément, their role is suspected but is not stated openly. In IV, i, the third subsidiary theme enters with Carduche. It, like the other two, constitutes an unknown quantity in the developing action. All this means that the process of the convergence of seemingly unconnected motives toward the distant point of the denouement becomes an absolute necessity. This effect of the interweaving of separate plots is also aided by having one scene deal with two threads of the story at the same time. The plot scheme indicates that this occurs a number of times. All this suggests that Hardy was thinking of the plot as a unit made up of parts that were so thoroughly fused that they came to form an indivisible whole. He conceived the present dramatic work, therefore, in the Baroque terms of amorphous plot masses rather than the distinct and well-defined lines that characterize the single plot of the typical Renaissance tragedy.[2]

A point of difference between the settled practice of the Spanish *comedia* and that of the present play should be suggested here. Whereas the *comedia* regularly conducted all the elements to a fusion at the end, Hardy suddenly drops the stories of Clément-Précieuse and Andrès-Carduche after they have served their purpose. These elements are used simply to complicate the plot, and the Spanish habit of causing all the motives to focus on the ending was either not understood by Hardy or else he merely elected to use a different process of plot development. This, of course, does not militate against the final fusion of the theme of Andrès-Précieuse with that of Ferdinand-Guiomar-Précieuse. It is typical of the Baroque feeling in these matters that the denouement, although it has been hinted at since the first appearance of Précieuse's parents in II, iii, is intended to be a surprise and is disclosed with startling suddenness in the last few scenes.

An examination of the various themes shows that they are characterized by a restless and continuous movement, and by contrast. The play is never allowed to settle into the comfortable jog-trot of the Renaissance play in its measured movement toward an inevitable goal. Instead, the line of the story jumps nervously from one subject to another. In the first acts, only two consecutive scenes (I, ii and II, i) treat of the same motive. The course of the story is kept in a state of chronic imbalance as successive scenes appear to push the outcome now in one direction and now in another. The constant vacillation of the course of action sets up strong contrastive values between the sharply differentiated outcomes that are thereby suggested. First, it becomes clear that Andrès wants Précieuse and then it is evident that Clément has the same objective in mind. The same kind of opposed possibilities arises in a Renaissance play, of course, but they are not presented with the Baroque will to a sharp, deliberate contrast that is so well served by causing events to favor first one outcome and then another. The abruptness of these plot contrasts is illustrated by the sudden entry of a new element as late as IV, i, when Carduche's interference gives a different direction to the story and seems to threaten Andrès with sudden destruction. In this case, as in others where the plot undergoes a sudden deflection, the will to contrast in plot elements is unmistakable.

In the management of the plot, an obviously logical development is avoided in favor of the roundabout method implied in the rapid movement of the several motives. The opening scene is built around the central theme but it gives no hint as to how it will end. I, ii introduces a new element in the person of Don Sancho, who intends to attempt to win Précieuse for himself. The role of Ferdinand and Guiomar is hinted at on their first appearance in II, iii but remains largely uncertain until Act V. By the beginning of Act IV, the situation is thoroughly confused and the outcome is made still more uncertain by the incident of the plot of Andrès-Carduche that is suddenly introduced in this act. Only as late as V, iii does the old gypsy woman's monolog suggest that the denouement will be a happy one. But not even yet is the author prepared to direct the story to its ending. The following scene intrudes a distracting element in Andrès' soliloquy on the imminent death that apparently awaits him. The pause here constitutes a brief suspension of the action before the fast-moving denouement in the following scenes. From V,v on to the final scene, the movement becomes more and more vertiginous as first Guiomar and then Ferdinand, Précieuse, and Andrès are informed of the good fortune that has come to them. It is characteristic that the successive revelations to each of these personages is abrupt and surprising. This sudden disclosure, as opposed to a full knowledge of the plot from the beginning, as in the Renaissance theater, is motivated by a wish to avoid the logical management of action, as well as by the desire to attain an extreme rapidity of plot development.

The presence of the three tributary plots acts effectively to divert attention from the principal subject. The long descriptions and discussions of matters of current interest that are common in the Spanish *comedia*, however, are not found here. Insofar as concerns seemingly irrelevant soliloquies, two occur in the present work—that of Don Sancho in I, ii and the one spoken by Andrès in V, iv. The decorative passages of the *comedia* appear therefore to be present in Hardy's play but to be noticeably less profuse and less pronounced than in the Spanish drama.

There are obviously more plots and characters than are strictly necessary to conduct the story to its end, although there are just enough to allow its presentation in the Baroque manner. The Renaissance author would have felt it mandatory to reduce the number of plots and characters to a minimum, while Hardy as a Baroque playwright deemed it equally necessary to increase the number of both for the sake of the ensuing complexity. The relations between the various motifs tend to be uncertain until near the end of the play. In this respect as well as in the other qualities of the plot, Hardy's *La belle égyptienne* seems to be thoroughly Baroque.

STYLE

In the matter of the conformations of the language, Baroque characteristics lie ready to hand. In I, i (p. 115, ll. 61–62), there occurs this metaphor, spoken by Précieuse in defense of virtue:

> L'or se prise affiné dans l'ardente fournaise,
> Non la victoire acquise ocieuse et à l'aise.

The first line contains the familiar and ordinary figure of gold refined in the furnace. The second line assumes that a victory in the battle for virtue belongs to the same class as the refined gold, whereas in reality a victory is not capable of being refined. The peculiarity to which attention is directed here is that Hardy makes a sudden jump from one kind of comparison to another of a completely different order without any

transitional preparation. The hearer is expected to instantaneously supply
the necessary link between the two terms of the metaphor, and indeed
there is no difficulty in doing so. But the sharp distinction between this
stylistic procedure and that of the Renaissance is obvious. Under the
earlier ideal of stylistic beauty, the figure of speech was developed in a
leisurely manner and abrupt transferrals of this nature were unknown.
Another metaphor of much the same kind is used in IV, iv (p. 142, ll.
63–65). Précieuse feels a presentiment of evil to come and she says:

> Vn trouble merueilleux m'agite le cerueau,
> Ainsi que le nocher appréhende sur l'eau
> Trop de calme annonçant la tempeste outrageuse
> Qui mesle dans le ciel vne mer orageuse . . .

The use of the transitional 'ainsi' is reminiscent of the Renaissance
mode but at the same time the form has become less stiff and is no
longer fixed in the rigid structure of 'Comme . . . ainsi . . .' that is
common in the Renaissance style, as has been remarked elsewhere in
the present monograph.

In one respect, at least, a trait of the sixteenth century seems to have
passed more or less intact into the theater of the later period; that is to
say, the interest in Greek and Roman literature is still vigorous. This
awareness of the ancient literatures finds expression in *La belle égyptienne*
in an unending torrent of references to Greek and Latin mythology,
history, and literature. Two examples from among many will illustrate. In I, i (p. 117, ll. 49–50), Précieuse says to Andrès:

> Tenez, mon Caualier, la parole auancée
> D'une pauure Andromède inuincible Persée.

And in V, iii (p. 152, ll. 55–56), the old gypsy addresses herself in this
fashion:

> Tu pourrois consulter les vieus chênes d'Epire,
> Ou Prothée contraint dedans l'humide empire . . .

It may be remarked in passing that these lines show the same lack of concern with a realism of cause and effect that is found in the Baroque in Spain. Under a nineteenth-century concept of art, it would be a foolish anomaly to put a classical reference into the mouth of an ignorant old gypsy. Under the governance of the patterns of the seventeenth century, however, no contradiction is involved, since the feeling for a scientific adjustment to environment has not yet come into sight in the world of art.

A further Renaissance quality is the absence of marked deviations from the normal syntactical order and of puns. The Baroque habit of expressing contradictory ideas in parallel forms occurs only a few times and then rather briefly. In IV, iii (p. 142, ll. 45–48), Andrès tells Carduche that he cannot accept her offer:

> Andrès
> La parolle me lie autre part engagée.
> Carduche
> Ton mieux trouué t'absout à mon suiet changée.
> Andrès
> Oncques irréuocable elle ne changera.
> Carduche
> Par ainsi ta misère onc ne s'étrangera.

In V, ii (p. 150, ll. 27–31), Précieuse asks Guiomar to intercede for Andrès:

> Guiomar
> Le meurtre n'eut iamais excuse légitime.
> Précieuse
> Mais le mort agresseur a prouoqué ce crime.
> Guiomar
> Tout homicide encourt le suplice mortel.
> Précieuse
> Contraint, aucune loy ne l'approuuera tel.
> Guiomar
> Tu parles de faueur et selon ta cruelle.

The emotional repetition of a word or phrase is rare in the present play, although it does occur. In V, v (p. 154, l. 40), Guiomar says, 'Iamais iamais l'effet ne manque à ma parolle.' A few lines below (p. 155, l. 62), she says, 'Celuy même celuy que tenez en prison...'

It is pertinent to the present investigation of style to remark that in *La belle égyptienne* the vocabulary is no longer the restricted, conventional one of the Renaissance tragedy. The lexicon of Hardy's period included a large repertory of everyday words and technical expressions that would have been avoided by earlier playwrights as unsuited to the serious drama. In III, v (p. 136, l. 51), the term 'sa mine s'évente' is a part of military language. In I, i (p. 112, ll. 21–22), there occurs a line so boldly plebeian in terminology that it would have repelled the tragedian of the sixteenth century, especially since the nobly born hero uses it in reference to the supposed ancestry of the beautiful heroine. Don Jean says:

> Celuy qui dans les lacs de sa beauté me lie,
> D'vn vulgaire passant la plus fangeuse lie...

A few lines below (ll. 31–32), Don Jean, still speaking of Précieuse, says:

>   ... et rare diamant
> Se va dans ce fumier attaché diffamant.

In addition to their usefulness in indicating the wider and more varied vocabulary that is possible in the Baroque theater, these passages also illustrate the prominence of the element of contrast in the depiction of character. The evident intent here is to create an obvious opposition between Précieuse's innocent charm and the depravity of the gypsies among whom she lives. In thus opposing the sublime and the pure to the vulgar and the filthy, Hardy is apparently seeking the shock value to be found in sharp contrasts, which he felt, in common with his contemporaries in Spain, to be attractive for itself.

In III, iv (p. 135, ll. 25–29), Andrès expresses his faith in Précieuse's chastity in terms of extravagant contradictions:

> Le Cigne du corbeau vêtira le plumage
> Philomelle au hibou donnera son ramage,
> L'Océan desséché regrettera ses eaus,
> La plante de Bacchus haïra les ormeaus
> Premier que ma déesse ingratte me trahisse . . .

The examination of a number of plays previous to the present one has demonstrated that, with a few exceptions, the use of humor did not fall within the range of the serious play of the sixteenth century, whether tragedy or tragi-comedy. In *La belle égyptienne*, however, humor has become an accepted part of the serious drama. The first remark made by Précieuse is a sarcastic observation on Don Jean's paleness. She says I, i (p. 112, ll. 65–66):

> O la belle rencontre! ô l'heureuse embuscade!
> Cette paleur pourtant le montre vn peu malade.

In I, i (p. 118, ll. 89–92), the old gypsy woman testily informs Précieuse that she has nothing to learn from a young girl about how to get money from rich men:

> L'amour plus que la peur de perdre te maîtrise,
> A plumer ces pigeons encore mal apprise,
> Qui ne viennent après que mieus au colombier,
> Simple tu me veus donc apprendre mon métier?

In II, ii (p. 126, ll. 61–62), Don Jean expresses his conception of becoming a gypsy in these terms:

> A devenir pratic en manière de prendre,
> D'emprunter des voisins, et de ne iamais rendre . . .

In III, ii (p. 131, ll. 95–96), a gypsy refers to the lesson that has undoubtedly been driven home to Clément, who has been badly chewed by the gypsies' dogs:

> [Il] A de male fortune eprouué de nouueau
> Que nos chiens ont les dents plus dures que sa peau . . .[3]

By this time (1615–20), therefore, the use of the comic has been thoroughly established in the serious drama in France. In this connection, a comparison with the contemporary Spanish *comedia* should be of some profit as a mutual illumination of the dramatic art in the two countries. The humor in Hardy's play is relatively muted and less elaborate than in the *comedia*. It is significant that whereas the *gracioso* is an established feature of the Spanish theater, no comparable character occurs in the play now under investigation. It may be suggested that this difference is indicative of a stronger influence of the Renaissance than was the case in Spain. The trend of the Spanish drama in another direction than the one it took in France may be set down tentatively to the relative weakness of the Renaissance in that country.[4]

In the study of the language of *La belle égyptienne*, it has been possible to observe the typically Baroque qualities of extravagance, contrast, and humor. It is noticeable, however, that the far-fetched conceit à la Góngora is completely missing in Hardy's play. The emotional tone, on the other hand, is strictly in line with Baroque practices. The first speech of the play, a monolog by Don Jean, establishes an atmosphere of personal feeling, of intense but soft emotion that can be contrasted with the majestic impersonality of the Renaissance on the one hand and on the other with the languorous softness of the Rococo that will be foreshadowed in Racine's *Phèdre*. The extravagance of feeling and expression that is found in the plastic arts of the time is embodied in a speech by Don Jean. In I, i (p. 116, ll. 5–10), he tells what he would be willing to do in order to win Précieuse:

> Quand tu proposerois à ma flamme ignorée
> Les périls encourus pour la Toison dorée

Du preus Thessalien, ou ces trauaus hardis
Qui mirent dans l'Olympe vn Alcide iadis,
Ma dextre entreprendroit sous le Dieu qui l'anime
D'égaler à peu près leur gloire magnanime . . .

In addition to illustrating the Baroque extravagance of emotion, this passage has as well a certain instructive value concerning the survival of vestiges of the previous period in an essentially Baroque context. Just as the churches of this period show Doric, Ionic, and Corinthian columns covered with a profuse decoration, in the same way the references to the ancient classical tradition, which have been funneled through the Renaissance, are embedded in a Baroque form and exist in a Baroque emotional atmosphere.

Another scene that embodies the strong feeling of the Baroque is the conversation that Andrès has with Clément in III, v (pp. 135–37). The tension of this scene, in which Andrès knows Clément as a rival but is not known as such by Clément, is deliberately prepared for in Andrès' monolog, which immediately precedes. In IV, vii, the feeling of the play is raised to a high level through the use of physical violence. The passage in which the soldier slaps Andrès and is then killed reads as follows (p. 147, ll.15–22):

Soldat

. . . .
Ton vol se void, se touche, ah! ma colère échape,
Et faut que cette joue impudente ie frape.
Précieuse
Quoy? sur le magistrat entreprendre à ses yeux?
Il n'y a plus pour nous de iustice en ces lieus.
Andrès
Téméraire, ton sang me lauera l'outrage,
Tu sçauras que l'habit n'empêche le courage.
Soldat
A l'aide, mes amis, à l'aide, ie suis mort,
Ne laissez impuny cet homicide effort.

The function of violent action to increase tension is clear enough here and is diametrically opposed to the practice of the Renaissance in this respect. At the same time, it must be pointed out that emotion is not exploited throughout the entire work to such an extent as is common in the Spanish *comedia*. By the end of the play, however, the intensity of feeling has been raised to a pitch that is comparable to that of the Spanish theater, and it appears to be managed with the same careful eye to the exploitation of strong feeling. In the use of emotion, therefore, Hardy appears to have objectives and techniques that coincide passably with those of the Spanish theater. The difference between them is that in the *comedia* the emotion is often religious in nature, while in *La belle égyptienne* the atmosphere is entirely secular.

CHARACTERS

The predilection for contrast and ambiguity of relationships that are apparent in the plot can also be seen operating in the characters. In two cases, those of Andrès and Clément, there occurs a sharp contrast between the characters and the circumstances under which they find themselves. Both are gentlemen who abandon their accustomed mode of life in order to follow Précieuse and who for her sake live with a band of thievish gypsies to whom honesty and honor are unknown. This opposition between gypsies and gentlemen is repeatedly pointed up by referring to the gypsies as rascals, as Ferdinand does in V, i (p. 148, ll. 55–58):

> L'exemple me suffit d'vne race méchante
> Qui l'oreille et les yeus du populaire enchante,
> Qui vole, qui saccage, errant où sa fureur
> D'obstacle ne préuoit qui luy donne terreur . . .

The numerous remarks of this kind on the part of Clément, Andrès, and Guiomar, and the depiction of the old gypsy woman as a selfish old harridan, all act, whether consciously or unconsciously, on the part of the author as a means of strengthening the distinction between the gypsies on the one hand and those personages of a higher moral level on the other. In this connection, it is apropos to point out that the personality and activities of Clément seem to be opposed in much the same way to those of Andrès. It is apparent from the beginning that Andrès intends to marry Précieuse, while Clément wants merely to seduce her. His intentions are made clear in I, ii (p. 119, ll. 27–32):

> Chez elle me promet vn plus facile accès,
> Engagée au combat ie gagne mon procès,
> Soldat victorieus, vne actiue poursuite
> M'asseure la victoire, et soudain met en fuite
> Ces chimères d'honneur, qu'à force de raisons
> Sur l'heure disparoir aisément nous faisons.

In a typical Baroque fashion, the relationship between Andrès and Précieuse refuses to remain constant. At first, her attitude toward him is one of friendly mockery and she is often flippant or coquettish in contradistinction to the grave, precocious heroine of Cervantes' story. In I, i, Don Jean tells her that she has bound him with chains. She answers (p. 113, ll. 75–76):

> On traitte les poulains de la sorte au printemps,
> De peur que déchaînez ils ne gagnent les champs.

In III, iii (p. 133, ll. 61–62), she responds flirtatiously to a flattering remark from Andrès:

> Mocqueur, attends au moins que Précieuse absente
> Le subtil aiguillon de ta langue ne sente.

By the end of the play, however, she is seriously in love with him and is no longer disposed to ridicule him.

The character of Andrès, like that of Précieuse, has undergone a transformation in passing from a Spanish to a French medium of expression. In III, v (p. 137, ll. 74–76), he tells Clément that he is Précieuse's

I

brother, hoping in this way to trap Clément into some indiscretion. Andrès, whom Cervantes conceived as the soul of honesty and discretion, becomes cynical and suspicious of Précieuse's virtue. Toward the end of the play, the innate goodness of both is evident but the distinction between the French and the Spanish versions of the story is plain.

In order to locate these changeable attitudes in their proper perspective as constituent parts of a Baroque outlook, it is expedient to compare them with the static relations between Electra and Clytemnestra in Baïf's *Electra*, or between Hippolytus and Phaedra in Garnier's *Hippolyte*. This whole bizarre (i.e., non-Renaissance) quality of Andrés' strange situation as it affects both action and personality is summarized in a speech by Guiomar in V, v (p. 155, ll. 61–66), which reads in part as follows:

> Vn ieune Caualier et d'antique maison
> Celuy même celuy que tenez en prison,
> Deuint éperdu'ment amoureus de ma fille,
> Emporte ce qu'il peut à sa riche famille,
> Et dessous vn espoir d'hyménée promis
> A l'infâme métier des Bohèmes s'est mis . . .

It is interesting to observe that the conception of the hero and heroine in *La belle égyptienne* points toward a spirit of rationalism in Hardy as opposed to the religious-theological approach of Cervantes to the problem of the relationship between the sexes. In *La gitanilla*, both Andrés and Preciosa represent Christian sexual virtue as it presented itself to seventeenth-century Spain, characterized by loyalty and chastity and by sexual relations only within the limits prescribed by the Church. Andrès, although he has all these desirable qualities in *La belle égyptienne*, is touched with the spirit of suspicion and cynicism. Hardy's Précieuse has all the expected virtues but at the same time she is flippant and flirtatious. The French Andrès has an exclusive desire for joy in this world that is markedly at variance with the Spanish outlook of the time In I, i (p. 114, ll. 17–21), he says to Précieuse:

Ta diuine beauté me dérobe à moy-même,
Te seruir me tient plus content qu'vn Diadème,
Ma fortune à tes pieds se prosterne, qui veus,
N'auoir d'orénauant autre saint à mes voeus,
N'auoir autre désir, n'auoir autre pensée . . .

His soliloquy as he lies in jail waiting for his certain death is concerned with this world rather than the next. He says in part V, iv (p. 152, ll. 83–90):

La Parque inéuitable ores ne m'épouuante,
Ma constance à bon droit inuincible se vante,
Le glorieus sujet qui cause mon trépas
Luy charme sa douleur à ce funèbre pas,
Hélas! qu'un seul regret ie n'emporte du monde,
Ma Carite laissée à iamais vagabonde,
Pauure de biens, d'amis, de capable suport
Qui puisse en mieus changer la rigeur de son sort . . .

At such a critical moment, with the hero expecting to be hanged at any moment, the Spanish Baroque theater would have been sure to introduce into a soliloquy some reflections of a moral and religious nature. The preoccupation of Andrès' monolog with the affairs of this world is to be contrasted with Segismundo's speech under similar conditions in Calderón's *La vida es sueño* (ll. 103–72), where he speaks at length of justice and liberty. It may also be of some value to the understanding of the differences between the Spanish and French theaters to place Andrès' boast of fearlessness before death beside Rodrigue's swaggering after his victory over the Moors. Back of these attitudes in both *Le Cid* and *La belle égyptienne*, there lies a common indifference to the religious questions that still trouble Spain. Evidently France has been more open to the currents of changing opinion than has Spain and has been profoundly influenced in philosophy and religion by the rising scientific spirit as well as by the bitter religious conflicts of the preceding century. Spain, on the other hand, has already closed herself off from any communication with these ideological transformations and has deliberately allowed herself to petrify into the older molds. It is to this difference in outlook that the more rationalistic tone of the French theater is to be attributed. This is the reason for the presence in the seventeenth-century French drama of generalized moral attitudes rather than the specifically Catholic teachings that are frequently found in the Spanish theater.

In addition to this alienation from religion, the French theater has another new attitude toward life which it shares with the Spanish *comedia*. All pretence toward the high-flown heroism of the Renaissance has disappeared. This feeling for the heroic, which persisted at least through the time of Garnier's *Bradamante* (1582), has given way to a bourgeois world in which the heroic ideal of the sixteenth century is incomprehensible. Even in *Le Cid*, Corneille manages to reconcile the demands of filial obligation with those of love in a way that satisfies the imperative of duty at the same time that it fulfils the protagonist's desire for happiness. The values of these new times are those of love, money, and position rather than those of the high resolve and devotion to duty of the Renaissance. This change is reflected in the present play in the choice of contemporary life as the subject, with an element of romantic exoticism furnished by the gypsies.

In general, the secondary characters serve only to make Andrès and Précieuse stand out vividly against the background that they furnish. The process by which this is done is peculiar to the dramatic art of the seventeenth century; that is to say, some of the merely tributary characters at times display their own idiosyncrasies of personality that would in the previous period have been considered irrelevant. This quality is particularly striking in the cases of Clément, the old gypsy woman, and Carduche. In I, ii, Clément in his first appearance has the stage to himself for a soliloquy. In II, i, he shows himself to be skilled in repartee with a pretty girl. In I, i and III, i, the old gypsy woman makes felt the astringent bitterness of her personality. In V, iii, she makes a display of her cunning. Carduche temporarily acquires the same kind of prominence in a monolog in IV, i. This habit of causing the secondary personages to gravitate momentarily to the forefront of attention is to be contrasted with the earlier custom of maintaining a rigid and permanent distinction between primary and secondary characters. In Hardy's play, the practice is not carried to the extreme that is often the case in the Spanish *comedia*, but the difference is one of degree rather than of kind.

Where the relationships of the several characters are concerned, there seems to be nothing like the numerous cross-relations that grow up during the course of a work like *La vida es sueño*. All the secondary personages seem to be grouped around Andrès and Précieuse and to be related only to them rather than having connections among themselves. As has been the case with other qualities of *La belle égyptienne*, this may be set down tentatively to the continuing influence of the Renaissance attitudes toward art. The earlier artistic pattern appears to function to delay the drift toward the later one.

This examination of Hardy's *La belle égyptienne* suggests that it is essentially Baroque in both form and ideology. To a limited extent in its structure and much more noticeably in its general view of life, it differs from the contemporary Spanish theater. This is not intended to imply that Hardy's work is any the less Baroque but merely that it is of a different kind of Baroque.

Notes

[1] The edition used is as follows: Alexandre Hardy, *Le théâtre d'Alexandre Hardy Parisien*, ed. E. Stengel (Marburg, 1884), V, 110–59. The division into scenes is by the present writer, since the division in this edition often fails to indicate a change in the course of the plot. Subsequent references to *La belle égyptienne* will be indicated only by giving the number of the act, scene, page, or line as the case may be. The system of accentuation has been modernized in all passages quoted herein.

[2] The amorphous quality of the color masses in Baroque painting can be observed in Velasquez' 'Venus with the Mirror' (Fig. 14). In the figure of Venus, the line of her hair is only vaguely defined against the curtains. Her back, instead of being delineated with a definite line, shades off gradually into the color of the cloth on which she is lying. The dark frame of the mirror lacks any sharp definition against the hangings behind it, as does the body of Cupid. Holbein's 'Edward VI when Prince of Wales' (Fig. 15) illustrates the Renaissance dependence on line rather than on masses of color with indeterminate edges. The back of the prince's head is in shadow but this does not obscure in any degree the clearness of the outline of the head against the blue background. In the same way, the profile of the face is drawn with a hard, firm line. Even such unpromising objects as the feather and the ermine trim are conceived and executed in strictly linear terms. The governance of the line is visible at every point. At this juncture, it is apropos to direct attention once more to Titian's 'Venus of Urbino' (Fig. 12). The epochal contrast between this nude and the one by Velasquez becomes even more pronounced by virtue of the similarity in subject matter coupled with the radical differences in the rendering of the forms.

[3] An evident typographical error in the text has been corrected here. The edition used reads, 'Que nos chien sont . . .'

[4] The weakness and brevity of the Renaissance spirit in the plastic arts of Spain is notorious. The Renaissance attitude toward art seems to have been largely incompatible with the Spanish temperament and readily gave way to Mannerism and the Baroque. The strong revulsion which Spain came to feel against the Reformation may also have been at work to influence art in the new direction.

6

Corneille, *Le Cid* (1637)[1]

SUMMARY OF PLOT

The Count, Chimène's father, insults Don Diègue, Rodrigue's father. Rodrigue challenges the Count to a duel and kills him. Although she and Rodrigue are in love, Chimène is obliged to try to bring about his death. She appeals to the king but before Rodrigue can be brought to trial the Moors attack. Rodrigue leads a band of soldiers and defeats the Moors. The king then decides that Rodrigue, whom the Moors now call the Cid, will engage in a duel with Chimène's champion. The winner in the battle is to take Chimène as his wife. She chooses Don Sanche to fight for her but tells Rodrigue that she wants him to win. Rodrigue defeats Sanche by disarming him and the king tells Chimène that she must marry Rodrigue after a suitable period of mourning for her father.

PLOT SCHEME

Rodrigue the knight	Rodrigue-Chimène	Infanta-Rodrigue-Chimène	Sanche-Rodrigue-Chimène	Comte-Diègue
		Act I		
i			i	
		ii		
				iii
				iv
v				v
vi	vi			

Rodrigue the knight	Rodrigue-Chimène	Infanta-Rodrigue-Chimène	Sanche-Rodrigue-Chimène	Comte-Diègue
		Act II		
				i
ii				
	iii	iii		iii
iv	iv			
		v		
				vi
				vii
	viii			viii
		Act III		
	i			
			ii	
	iii			
iv	iv			
				v
vi	vi			
		Act IV		
i	i			
ii	ii	ii		
iii				
	iv			
	v		v	
		Act V		
i	i			
ii		ii		
		iii		
	iv			
	v		v	
vi	vi		vi	
vii	vii			

PLOT

It has been remarked that the Baroque thought of plot in terms of the fusion and interweaving of several elements, whereas the Renaissance used one motive only, with a consequent impossibility of fusing several of them. An examination of the plot scheme given indicates to what an extent Corneille went in this respect. There are no fewer than five themes, among which the several scenes are distributed in a highly complex manner. Nor is this complexity simply a matter of aimless wandering among tributary affairs until the denouement can be brought about. There is at all points a careful interweaving of the various parts. This is evident, among other things, in the fact that a number of scenes deal with two or more plots at the same time, which occurs with sufficient frequency to suggest that it is done purposefully. A single example will serve to illustrate. In Act II, scene vii, the king's remark to the effect that ten enemy vessels have been observed on their way up the river prepares for the later appearance of the Moors. Here, in a scene devoted to one theme (Comte and Diègue), a future event related to a second motive (Rodrigue the knight) is anticipated, and two scenes are joined with unobtrusive forethought.

Throughout the course of the play, the themes are made to run parallel, often with a seeming lack of connection between one theme and the others. But at the same time, the course of the action is suggested early in the play and is kept before the audience almost constantly. In the first two scenes, it seems that the principal motive is to be the triangle of Rodrigue, Chimène, and the Infanta. This is, in fact, not precisely true, and it is necessary to wait until scene vi before it is disclosed that the story is really concerned only with the love of Rodrigue and Chimène, and the consequent conflict of love and honor within each of them. After scene vi, however, the audience could at any point throughout the rest of the work state confidently the nature of its chief subject. From this point on, a single motive exercises a strong domination over the story and toward the end of the play draws the other plots into itself and absorbs them. This process of convergence has a peculiar characteristic, however, that must be carefully noted. As the plot scheme demonstrates, the theme of the Count and Diègue, which is of considerable prominence in the first three acts, disappears by III, v. This motive, instead of merging with that of Rodrigue-Chimène, simply ceases to exist. In V, iii, the Infanta ceases to compete for Rodrigue's favors and relinquishes him to Chimène. This means that out of the five plots that go to make up the action of *Le Cid*, only three actually undergo the dense unification typical of the Baroque theater.

The avoidance of a logical development of action is visible at many points. After the play has run its course and time has been had for calm afterthought, the significance of a speech by Chimène becomes plain enough. In I, ii, she says to Elvire:

> Il semble toutefois que mon âme troublée
> Refuse cette joie, et s'en trouve accablée:
> Un moment donne au sort des visages divers,
> Et dans ce grand bonheur je crains un grand revers.

These few lines contain the play in miniature and foreshadow its entire course, but this tendency toward clarity of plot exposition is checked and largely canceled out not only by its own vagueness but also by various distractions from the main line of action. Among these diversions can be mentioned the delay of full information concerning the principal theme until I, vi; the Infanta's wavering between love and duty; and Rodrigue's hesitation (in I, vi) before his manifest obligation to protect his father's honor. In III, iv, in the lines beginning 'Ah, Rodrigue . . .,' Chimène speaks in such a way that the audience is for several lines in doubt as to whether she will kill him or not. During Rodrigue's ensuing speech this uncertainty persists; it constitutes a momentary lack of clearness and is a departure from the insistence during the sixteenth century on an unremitting clarity at every point. In V, v, Sanche's entrance after his duel with Rodrigue constitutes another intervention of Baroque uncertainty. The audience has up to this moment been sufficiently certain that Rodrigue will be victorious, and indeed the present doubt endures for no more than a moment. But the crucial point here is that Corneille conceals the outcome and lets the issue hang fire for a time. This mode of presentation would have been unthinkable to a Renaissance author, who would have been careful to maintain an atmosphere of assurance concerning the outcome of the story.

An ideological equivalent of this uncertainty occurs in III, v, where Diègue refers to the uneasiness of the present life:

> Jamais nous ne goûtons de parfaite allégresse:
> Nos plus heureux succès sont mêlés de tristesse;
> Toujours quelques soucis en ces événements
> Troublent la pureté de nos contentements.
> Au milieu du bonheur mon âme en sent l'atteinte:
> Je nage dans la joie, et je tremble de crainte.

These lines are all the more remarkable in that they are perhaps the sole direct expression of a transcendental view of life in a play that is saturated with humanism. Diègue's uneasy consciousness that all earthly happiness leaves something to be desired implies a state of mind favorable to the next life and adversely critical of the present one. The similarity between the ideology here and that of a contemporary *comedia* is notable. The rarity of this otherworldly attitude in the present play suggests the breadth of the ideological gulf between Spain and France during the seventeenth century.

The liking for an oblique approach is also visible in the handling of Rodrigue's challenge of the Count in II, ii. Instead of defying him immediately and openly, he approaches the subject by indirection and stealth. The effect of this roundabout procedure is to sharply increase the emotional tension, for the audience knows what he intends to do and perceives that he is moving toward his purpose in some indirect way that is not yet known. The effect is to make the audience grow tense while awaiting the outcome. A similar encounter handled in direct fashion would, of course, produce emotional stress, but this is beside the point. The matter of principal concern here is to describe the form used by Corneille in developing this scene; his preference for indirectness is typically Baroque.

All these matters tend to impair the inevitable quality of the plot without yet pushing it to an extreme of uncertainty. *Le Cid* affords an example of the blending of various attitudes toward beauty held by both the sixteenth century, whose emotional and esthetic effects depended on inevitability, and the seventeenth, whose feeling for dramatic expressiveness rested on the element of theatrical surprise. Instances of the traditional procedure of a logical approach to the plot lie ready to hand. In I, ii, the Infanta says bluntly of Rodrigue, 'Je l'aime.' She then proceeds to explain concisely why she is determined to have Rodrigue marry Chimène even though she herself is in love with him. The argument between Don Fernand and Sanche concerning the punishment due the Count (II, vi) is characterized by a carefully reasoned approach to the problem and seems to be a part of a seventeenth-century rationalism that is a continuation of the logical tradition of sixteenth-century art. This careful reasoning is in sharp distinction to the more emotional and lyrical complexion of the Spanish *comedia* and of such French playwrights as Quinault. Rodrigue's insistence on explaining logically and at considerable length his motives for obeying the demands of honor rather than of love is a part of the author's bias toward an attitude regarding art that is sanctioned by the earlier tradition. Rodrigue succeeds even in justifying (in III, iv) his killing of the Count by asserting that he would otherwise not have been worthy of Chimène's love. This explanation of the necessity of preserving his honor is made by means of a carefully constructed argument.

The need for a rational justification of the course followed by the story is visible also in the explanation by the Infanta to Chimène that Rodrigue is now too valuable to the nation to allow her to continue seeking his death. The audience must not be allowed to think that the king's defense of Rodrigue is an arbitrary contrivance to which recourse is had in order to make the play come right at the end. It is to be remarked that Guillén de Castro uses a different device to make his hero of too great value to permit of his destruction, that is, he has him defeat the Moors repeatedly rather than just once. This, however, involves the lapse of considerable time and would, if used by Corneille, have constituted a deviation from the habit established by the Renaissance tragedy of reducing the time of the play to a minimum. This possibly serves to explain, at least in part, Corneille's use of Rodrigue's quick victory over the Moors as a means of persuading Chimène to moderate her demands. The persistence of Renaissance attitudes is evident, although they have now become a part of a pattern of artistic forms that is essentially different.

A comparison of *Le Cid* with *Las mocedades* is instructive in connection with the matter of the clear exposition of the story. In both plays, all incidents are designed to direct attention to the Cid, but the manner in which it is done is different in each case. The incidents of Corneille's play point at Rodrigue most of the time. The only scenes in which he does not have a prominent role, either through his presence on stage or through discussion by the other characters, are I, iii and II, i. In Guillén de Castro's work, the exaltation of Rodrigo is partly concealed until the latter portion of the work. In this matter, then, both plays are Baroque but *Le Cid* is the more conservative in its technique. Strangely enough, in spite of this constant pointing at Rodrigue in all but a few scenes, the intent to exalt him is not nearly so apparent as it is in Castro's work. This appears to be so because Corneille subtracted the religious meaning from the play and thereby cut the heart out of the theme of 'Rodrigo the Knight' without removing it entirely. *Las mocedades* is a work that concerns only Rodrigo and his religious-national significance, while *Le Cid* deals with the exclusively humanistic qualities of the love of the two principals, so that Chimène of necessity becomes of equal importance with Rodrigue and prevents an exclusive concentration on him.

It is this shift of the ideological center that transforms Rodrigue's fanfaronade (end of V, ii) into a pointless braggadocio that is incomprehensible and impertinent in a hero of the nature imputed to him in Corneille's play. The possible historical explanation of this passage as a surviving echo of the Spanish *romances*, while undoubtedly true enough, does not necessarily function at the same time as its esthetic apology. In this connection, it must be made sufficiently clear that *Le Cid* is not at any point to be thought of as an imitation of *Las mocedades* nor in any way inferior to it. It is everywhere a genuine creation of the hand and mind of its author. Corneille's independence of Castro is indicated by the fact that he made a number of changes in plot and character but at the same time preserved a Baroque artistic pattern, even in those cases where he has patently incurred no direct debt to the work of Guillén de Castro. There seems, in fact, to be no reason for any reluctance in admitting freely the artistic superiority of *Le Cid* over *Las mocedades*, even when due allowances are made for the defects in the former.[2]

The various plots are characterized by a continuous movement with reference to each other. The line of the story changes rapidly from one subject to another, so that the action is never allowed to settle into the leisurely march of the Renaissance play along a single well-marked path. Furthermore, the events of one theme constantly change or threaten to change the course of one or all of the others. The opportune entrance of the Moors and their defeat by Rodrigue has a profound effect not merely on the central story of Rodrigue-Chimène but also on the theme of Rodrigue the knight. The duel of the Count and Don Rodrigue unsettles the leading plot of Rodrigue-Chimène, since it is at once apparent that the course of true love cannot run smooth under the new circumstances.

It has been remarked that the Baroque sought strong contrasts as a part of its peculiar esthetic pattern. Such contrasts are not lacking in the plot of *Le Cid*. In Act III, scene iv, Rodrigue asks Chimène to kill him with his own sword and thus secure the revenge she is seeking. It would be difficult to conceive of a scene more filled with contradictions than this one. The hero seeks his own death at the hands of his sweetheart. Neither of them really wishes his death, for the Cid would prefer to live and marry Chimène, a consummation which she also most ardently desires. At the same time, Chimène must attempt with every means at her disposal to encompass the death of her father's murderer, though it is the greatest fear of her life that she will succeed. It adds an extra fillip of paradox that the sword that Rodrigue offers her is the weapon with which he has so recently done the Count to death. The bizarre, paradoxical nature of the corresponding scene in Guillén de Castro's *Las mocedades del Cid* (Act II, ll. 1106 ff) is in Corneille's play preserved intact in situation, emotional quality, structure, and linguistic style. Corneille even adds a detail that does not occur in Castro's play, since the weapon in *Las mocedades* is a dagger undistinguished by any special associations, while in *Le Cid* it is the sword that has been used to dispatch Chimène's father. Corneille, in this one matter at least, goes farther even than Castro's intensely Baroque work.

The qualities of powerful contrast and emotional tension find expression yet elsewhere in *Le Cid*. In V, iv, Corneille devotes an entire scene to a discussion by Chimène and Elvire of the possible outcome of the duel between Rodrigue and Sanche. The only possibilities that they envisage are that one must win and the other will be killed. To a critic whose thoughts are fixed on the clear and logical handling of plot, this scene might seem to have the appearance of a mere filler that is used only because it allows time for the duel to take place. That is, to one who thinks in terms of a Renaissance clarity of plot, it would be meaningless or would best partake of the nature of an unnecessary padding of the skeleton of the story. Such is far from being the case. In point of fact, the scene has its use in the unfolding action and even becomes indispensable if considered from the Baroque viewpoint in these matters. This scene acts to raise emotional tension to a much higher pitch than would have been possible without it. Under the sly urging of the dialog between the two women, the audience unconsciously comes to accept the proposition that either Rodrigue or Sanche must be killed. In these circumstances, they are simply waiting for the conqueror to enter and claim Chimène, and the entrance of Sanche carrying a sword is a paralyzing shock. The spectators' first thought, of course, is that Rodrigue is dead. Lengthier reflection would make it clear that such a course of plot development is impossible, but to one who is participating in the action as it evolves and who accords to the author the indispensable imaginative co-operation, such reflection is hardly possible. Indeed Corneille has deliberately and for his own (esthetic) reasons made sure that this should be so, since he is in the process of creating a dramatic work in obedience to the need for contrast and emotional tension. Here, he makes a deliberate effort to achieve those extreme theatrical effects that have been the object of extensive contumely on the part of those more conservative critics who adhere to the orthodox canon of esthetic, compounded of equal parts of ancient Greek classicism, the Renaissance, and nineteenth-century positivistic realism. Although it means flying in the face of revealed doctrine in these matters, it seems necessary to point out that nothing could be further removed from a Renaissance procedure than this entrance by Sanche. In view of these considerations, it is possible to say that throughout the play there constantly recurs a powerful emotional state often bordering on hysteria that is highly characteristic of the Baroque and proportionately far removed from the rationalism, dignity, and propriety that are distinctive features of the sixteenth-century position in relation to questions of art.

One of the prominent traits of the Baroque theater is a superabundance of plots and characters. It is not intended to suggest that this superfluity is useless nor that it is prejudicial to the esthetic excellence of a given literary work. This abundance is an excess only in the fact that their numbers go beyond the minimum demands of the exposition of the story. *Le Cid*, in this respect as in others, is created in accordance with a conception of dramatic art that is both personal and epochal. As the plot scheme indicates, there are more themes and actors than are required by considerations of the development of the action. At the same time, it is apparent that it is not a question of an extreme Baroque style, in view of the tendency to restrict the personages to a smaller number than is usually found in the *comedia*.

STYLE

In the convolutions of the language of *Le Cid*, it is possible to observe in operation the same traits of contrast already elaborated on. The exploitation of the liking for opposites can be seen in the reduced compass of a brief phrase. In I, ii, Léonor refers to the Infanta's love for Rodrigue as '. . . un mal si doux et si cuisant . . .' The reference to love as an evil that is at once sweet and painful involves a contrast that is so plain that he who runs may read. A similar opposition occurs in a speech by Chimène in III, iv. She warns Rodrigue that she is obliged to avenge her father if it is possible to do so. In the last line of this speech, there is found the familiar paradox, by means of which the effect of all that has been so earnestly said is rendered null and void: 'Mon unique souhait est de ne rien pouvoir.'

In V, v, Corneille again reduces a complex set of contrastive situations to a small compass. Chimène, in speaking of Rodrigue's supposed death at Sanche's hand, says:

> Un même coup a mis ma gloire en sureté,
> Mon âme au désespoir, ma flamme en liberté.

Here, the dense nexus of contrasts is grouped around the fact that a single blow, in killing Rodrigue, has produced such a number of disparate effects that are mutually contradictory. Now that the Baroque metaphor in *Le Cid* has been examined in the small, a more extended figure of speech may be investigated. In III, iii, Chimène develops the figure of a battle in her heart between Rodrigue and her father.

> C'est peu de dire aimer, Elvire: je l'adore;
> Ma passion s'oppose à mon ressentiment;
> Dedans mon ennemi je trouve mon amant;
> Et je sens qu'en dépit de toute ma colère,
> Rodrigue dans mon coeur combat encor mon père:
> Il l'attaque, il le presse, il cède, il se défend,
> Tantôt fort, tantôt foible, et tantôt triomphant;
> Mais en ce dur combat de colère et de flamme,
> Il déchire mon coeur sans partager mon âme;
> Et quoi que mon amour ait sur moi de pouvoir,
> Je ne consulte point pour suivre mon devoir:

K

Je cours sans balancer où mon honneur m'oblige.
Rodrigue m'est bien cher, son intérêt m'afflige;
Mon coeur prend son parti; mais malgré son effort,
Je sais ce que je suis, et que mon père est mort.

Here, the metaphor of the battle in her heart is developed in considerable detail. It is true enough that the sixteenth-century trope often
runs to a considerable length, but there is a fundamental difference
between the Renaissance style and the mode of metaphorical elabora-
tion in the case under consideration. This extended figure seems to fit
perfectly Gracián's definition of the 'conceit' as a connection between
startlingly disparate objects. The relation between the heart and a battle-
ground is not impossible to the earlier style but it nevertheless lies off
the beaten track for it because of the soft, intimately personal emotion
that this implied comparison normally suggests. The figure of speech
is complex, elaborated at length, involves a metaphorical relationship
that would appear excessively physical to an artist of the sixteenth century, and would have seemed to the more rational playwright of that
earlier period almost morbid in its intensity. The esthetic purpose of
this almost shocking figure of speech, which is quite common in
Baroque literature, is to heighten the emotional impact on the audience.
No apology is meant and none is needed for either the Renaissance or
the Baroque manner in this connection. It is not that one is superior to
the other at any point but merely that they are different in their respective approaches to the creation of metaphorical speech. The fact that
these figures were taken from Guillén de Castro's *Las mocedades* does
nothing to contradict the argument concerning the Baroque qualities
of Corneille's play. The same liking for the juxtaposition of ideas that
ordinarily are not related can be seen also in Act II, scene viii, where
Chimène speaks to the king of her suffering over her father's death:

Sire, de trop d'honneur ma misère est suivie.
Je vous l'ai déjà dit, je l'ai trouvé sans vie;
Son flanc était ouvert; et pour mieux m'émouvoir,
Son sang sur la poussière écrivoit mon devoir;

> Ou plutôt sa valeur en cet état réduite
> Me parloit par sa plaie, et hâtoit ma poursuite;
> Et pour se faire entendre au plus juste des rois,
> Par cette triste bouche elle empruntoit ma voix.

Here, the act of writing is re-expressed in the startling terms of blood on a surface of dust. The metaphor that follows is even more extraordinary. The reference to a fresh wound as a mouth that speaks suggests to the audience an emotional state that borders on the hysterical and is not far removed from the morbid, all of which is of frequent occurrence in the theater of the schools of Lope and Calderón.

This settled habit of thinking of tropes in terms of startling, paradoxical, and even far-fetched conceits is evident again in Rodrigue's rejection of his father's suggestion that their joint honor is intact and that his love for Chimène can easily be diverted to someone else. Rodrigue says (III, vi), 'Mon honneur offensé sur moi-même se venge.' The contradictory turn of thought is apparent. One of the high points of paradox in both language and idea is reached in this exchange between the two principals in III, iv, where Rodrigue tries to persuade Chimène to take his sword and kill him:

> Don Rodrigue
> Regarde-le plutôt pour exciter ta haine,
> Pour croître ta colère, et pour hâter ma peine.
> Chimène
> Il est teint de mon sang.
> Don Rodrigue
> Plonge-le dans le mien . . .

A further contrast occurs in V, i, where Chimène finally asks Rodrigue to defeat Sanche for her sake. Against the grain of her sense of duty, she grudgingly requests what she has passionately desired all along; again, it is a case of paradox deliberately sought for. A similar quality of contrast is exploited in a speech by Chimène in V, iv. She expresses the need to choose between Sanche and Rodrigue in these terms:

Quoi! l'objet de ma haine ou de tant de colère!
L'assassin de Rodrigue ou celui de mon père!
De tous les deux côtés on me donne un mari
Encor tout teint du sang que j'ai le plus chéri . . .

This, like the other oppositions that have been cited, has reference to the prime contradiction of the play, the fact of her dilemma in having to choose either to leave her father unavenged or to bring about the Cid's death. In view of the fact that a work of art can hardly be regarded as a collection of fortuitous accidents, it is apparent that these contrastive effects are achieved in obedience to a feeling for art that is at least partly conscious.

The use of parallel forms to enclose mutually contradictory ideas appears with some frequency. In I, ii, Léonor expresses her pity for her mistress by saying, 'Je vous blâmais tantôt, je vous plains à présent . . .' It is characteristic of the Baroque style that this sentence not only encloses in the brief extent of a single line two opposing concepts, but that it also does so in a structural form that is peculiar to the seventeenth-century technique. That is, they are stated in two equally balanced halves that make use of a strictly parallel, grammatical construction, a form that has the effect of calling attention both to the structural forms and to the ideas which they enclose. In III, iii, Chimène mourns the death of her father in a speech that concludes with three lines which constitute a densely packed group of paradoxes:

La moitié de ma vie a mis l'autre au tombeau,
Et m'oblige à venger, après ce coup funeste,
Celle que je n'ai plus sur celle qui me reste.

Here again, the author plays off one conceptual element against another, balancing against each other the two 'halves of my life,' that is to say, Rodrigue and her father. The present critical intention is not merely to put into strong relief the opposing concepts of this passage but also to call attention to the structural forms that are employed to lend them their unique esthetic quality. These forms may be described in general terms as balanced and parallel parts that are used to point up a contrast of opposite ideas. These same esthetic ideals exercise a guiding influence in determining the artistic forms of another speech by Chimène a few lines below the one just quoted. She says:

> Et que dois-je espérer qu'un tourment éternel,
> Si je poursuis un crime, aimant le criminel?

Later in this same scene, Chimène remarks once more on the struggle within her soul between love and honor, making use of a compact series of balanced contrasts:

> Ma passion s'oppose à mon ressentiment;
> Dedans mon ennemi je trouve mon amant;
> Et je sens qu'en dépit de toute ma colère,
> Rodrigue dans mon coeur combat encor mon père;
> Il l'attaque, il le presse, il cède, il se défend,
> Tantôt fort, tantôt foible, et tantôt triomphant;
> Mais en ce dur combat de colère et de flamme,
> Il déchire mon coeur sans partager mon âme . . .

In I, ii, the Infanta says of the coming marriage of Rodrigue and Chimène:

> Je sens en deux partis mon esprit divisé:
> Si mon courage est haut, mon coeur est embrasé;
> Cet hymen m'est fatal, je le crains, et souhaite:
> Je n'ose en espérer qu'une joie imparfaite.
> Ma gloire et mon amour ont pour moi tant d'appas,
> Que je meurs s'il s'achève ou ne s'achève pas.

These lines are heavy with the usual Baroque oppositions stated in a brief, sententious manner and with a typically balanced form. In addition to all this, a further point concerning the present instance needs to be made, namely that the last line sums up the preceding argument in a dense contrast in which the two opposing ideas are stated with an extreme brevity in the familiar construction that uses equal half-lines.

This habit of restating a preceding pair of ideas in balanced form is a firmly settled one in the Baroque technique and recurs constantly in *Le Cid*. Rodrigue's soliloquy in I, vi is intensely Baroque in that it restates over and over the problem of love versus honor in paired and contrasting expressions or in lines that are paradoxical in nature. He says:

> Il faut venger un père et perdre une maîtresse:
> L'un m'anime le coeur, l'autre retient mon bras.
> Réduit au triste choix ou de trahir ma flamme,
>   Ou de vivre en infâme,
> Des deux côtés mon mal est infini.
>   O Dieu, l'étrange peine!
> Faut-il laisser un affront impuni?
> Faut-il punir le père de Chimène?

This established practice of stating opposed ideas in similar forms is expressed also in the habit of assigning to two different characters a series of brief speeches that function as alternating contrasts stated in strictly parallel structures. A passage of this sort occurs in the argument between Don Diègue and the Count in I, iii:

> Le Comte
> Ce que je méritois, vous l'avez emporté.
> Don Diègue
> Qui l'a gagné sur vous l'avoit mieux merité.
> Le Comte
> Qui peut mieux l'exercer en est bien le plus digne.
> Don Diègue
> En être refusé n'en est pas un bon signe.

Dialogs of this kind are commonplace in the theater of Lope and Calderón, where, as here, each pair of lines is mutually contradictory and closely parallel in form. Precisely the same kind of dialog occurs in the first few lines of II, viii, when Chimène and Don Diègue come to present their cases before the king. A similar pattern of contradictory speeches occurs in Diègue's soliloquy, in I, iv, where he rages against his impotence to avenge himself against the Count. Here, there is again a constant iteration of opposites like those already elaborated on, centered about the disparity between his present ineffectiveness and shame as opposed to his former power and honor.

Closely allied to this wish for paradox is the need for strong emotional tension. It is indeed one of the functions of contrast to excite this intensified feeling. In the scenes remarked upon above as possessing to an unusual degree this contrastive quality, one of their more conspicuous features is precisely the passion they reveal. Nor was this emotion lost on a contemporary audience. Documents of the time demonstrate that both the author of *Le Cid* and those who attended its performance were quite aware of the psychological effect intended. In this connection, Corneille remarks, '. . . alors que ce malheureux amant se présentait devant elle, il s'élevait un certain frémissement dans l'assemblée, qui marquait une curiosité merveilleuse, et un redoublement d'attention pour ce qu'ils avaient à se dire dans un état si pitoyable.'[3] It is also significant to note that the author of the anonymous *Jugement du Cid* refers approvingly to the strong feeling aroused by this scene in which Rodrigue asks Chimène to kill him.[4] The evidence, whether it be that afforded by contemporary comment or that of the forms of the play itself, all runs in one direction, to the effect that both Corneille and at least a part of his audience accepted certain Baroque qualities as being right and good, and in no way deserving of censure.

In all that has gone before, it has been evident that *Le Cid* at few points attains the Baroque principles with anything like the intensity and consistency observable in the Spanish *comedias* of the seventeenth century. These circumstances would seem to extend to the critic an opportunity to reproach Corneille's play for a putative inferiority to more faithfully consistent examples from the Spanish theater. This, however, would be wide of the mark. *Le Cid*, like any other work of art, must be accepted for what it is rather than being subjected to disparagement for what it might have been. The fact is that its style is that of a conservative variety of the Baroque and it must perforce be described as such. It is not deemed reprehensible in Poussin that he repeatedly combines in one picture the forms of the Baroque fused with obvious survivals from the sixteenth century.[5] In the same way, there seems to be no good reason for pointing the finger of shame at Corneille because he wrote a play that refuses to fall into line completely with the ideals of either the Spanish *comedia* or the Renaissance tragedy. Still less is there any defensible motive for a denial that the Baroque played a considerable part in the formation of Corneille's personal conception of art.

Although the preceding discussion has been concerned largely with various Baroque qualities, it is not the intention here to suggest that *Le Cid* is identical at all points with the Spanish *comedia*. In spite of the numerous undeniable similarities between the seventeenth-century theater in Spain and France, *Le Cid* frequently deals with problems of form in a way that denotes a somewhat different outlook on the creation of a dramatic work of art. The puns and the marked deviations from a normal word order, both of which are common in the *comedia*, are not used in *Le Cid*. The rather rigid form of the Alexandrine is to be contrasted with the much freer poetic system of the contemporary Spanish theater, with its octosyllabic line and the use of assonance rather than rhyme. The general view of life and of man's position in the universe also appears to be purely humanistic rather than transcendental, a matter whose understanding is facilitated by a consideration of the difference between *Las mocedades* and *Le Cid*. The objective of Castro's play is to exalt Rodrigo as the exemplary Christian knight. His purpose, in a word, is Catholic, Christian, and transcendental. Corneille, in obedience to a more rationalistic outlook, subtracted those elements that are religious in nature and produced a work grounded in purely human values.

CHARACTERS

Corneille's mode of viewing his characters indicates his orientation toward the forms of the Baroque, which no longer conceives of dramatic personality in terms of an imperturbable rigidity. Chimène is pulled between the forces of love and honor, of which love proves eventually to be the stronger. First, she is consumed by a desire to see Rodrigue dead, now she is in anguish for fear that her wish may be granted. She refuses Sanche's offer to kill Rodrigue (III, ii) and cannot kill him herself when he requests it (III, iv). She continues to pursue him but requires the goad of frequent self-reminders that her father must be avenged. Rodrigue himself suffers from this same desperate wish to be rid of his burdensome and exhausting conflict. All this creates an atmosphere of dynamic emotional tension that may be contrasted with the static quality of Orestes' unwavering assurance in Pérez de Oliva's *La venganza de Agamenón* (published 1528) as well as with that of Orestes in Baïf's *Electra*.[6] The inability of the Infanta to make up her mind whether she wants to marry Rodrigue or not is another case in point. In I, ii, she confesses to Léonor that she loves him and then immediately admits that such a feeling for him is unsuited to her high rank. The effect of this scene is not only to create a shifting relationship between Rodrigue and the Infanta but also at the same time to cast doubt on the possibility of a marriage between Rodrigue and Chimène. The chief ambiguity in these matters lies between Rodrigue and Chimène themselves. They begin as sweethearts but changing circumstances soon transform Rodrigue into the murderer of Chimène's father and Chimène into the would-be murderess of Rodrigue. It is significant of Corneille's essentially Baroque outlook in this respect that this bifurcate relation of lover-murderer persists until the end of the play and forms one of the chief sources of emotional tension and of the feeling of bizarre paradox.

The characters are treated in such a way that the minor figures at times acquire considerable prominence. One secondary plot, that of the Count and Don Diègue, is of such importance that it participates in no less than nine scenes. The four soliloquies in *Le Cid* are indicative of the tendency to place a considerable stress on the tributary personages. Of the four, Diègue is assigned two (I, iv and III, v), and the Infanta has one (V, ii), while Rodrigue speaks only one (I, vi). The Infanta is of secondary consequence in the story but she nevertheless has a satellite in the person of Léonor.

The relationships between the minor and major characters is equally revealing of a difference between the practices of the Renaissance and those of the work under consideration. The earlier esthetic demanded that the protagonists be related as an opposed pair and that each one should have in his wake a train of secondary figures, each of which should be related to one of the principals and to no one else. The Infanta, a lesser character, is connected not only with Rodrigue but also with Chimène. It is indicative of a Baroque outlook that she is related to each in two ways rather than one. To both, she occupies the position of the princess to whom they owe loyalty and obedience. At the same time, she wants to marry Rodrigue, and Chimène is consequently her rival. At the end of the play, as is inevitable, all these equivocal, shifting relations are resolved in the final exaltation of Rodrigue and Chimène, but the equivocal relations that have subsisted throughout the play among the characters prevent the attainment of the feeling of monumental simplicity that is so much a part of the Renaissance attitude in these matters. Here, as elsewhere, Corneille works under the influence of a conservative Baroque that has been affected by the ideals of the Renaissance tragedy.

In general terms, *Le Cid* embodies the esthetic forms and aspirations of an international Baroque style that governed the art of all of Europe during its period, with certain survivals from the Renaissance theater. More specifically, it is a personal expression of a peculiarly French variation on this multi-national pattern, into which various traits of the preceding era have been engrossed as part of the substance of a new conception of dramatic beauty.

For the most part, the criticism of the work now under consideration has strayed far from its proper path. The essential substance of this received critical opinion has found no more concise expression than it attains in this remark emanating from the Academy in its judgment of the *Cid* (1637): 'Enfin nous concluons qu'encore que le sujet ne soit pas bon, qu'il pêche dans son Desnouement, qu'il soit chargé d'Episodes inutiles, que la bienséance y manque en beaucoup de lieux . . .'⁷ In these observations, there is evidently to be understood an implied reference to Aristotle's laws of tragedy as fixed and immutable rules that should govern the course of the plot development in *Le Cid*. These preconceptions concerning the esthetic nature of Corneille's play have continued to color critical pronouncements down to the present time. Hence proceeds the easy assumption that *Le Cid* and other plays of the official theater of the time are 'Classical' in the Aristotelian sense. In spite of the frequent appeals to these ancient precepts as settled and universal laws of the drama, however, there is no apparent need to refer to Classical ideals for an explanation of the artistic concepts of the period in question.⁸ There is not and cannot be any such thing as the derivation of the living, active esthetic principles of one period from those of a remote previous epoch; this would be merely imitative rather than creative. A living, vigorous art form, such as the seventeenth-century theater in France, creates its own guiding principles. Any reference by artists or critics of that time to such a putative borrowing from ancient Greece is to be taken seriously only as an effort to lend the weight of tradition to independently developed articles of esthetic belief.

Notes

¹ The edition of *Le Cid* used here is as follows: Pierre Corneille, *Oeuvres de P. Corneille*, ed. Ch. Marty-Laveaux ('Les grands écrivains de la France', Paris, 1862), III, 3–241. Subsequent references to the text of *Le Cid* are to this edition unless otherwise specified and will be indicated only by giving the act, scene, or page number as the case may be.

² Some of the structural flaws of Guillén de Castro's play are discussed in Roaten and Sánchez y Escribano, *Wölfflin's Principles*, p. 151, note.

³ Pierre Corneille, *Théâtre complet de Corneille*, ed. Pierre Lièvre (n.p., n.d.), p. 567. The passage quoted is from Corneille's introduction to *Le Cid*.

⁴ H. C. Lancaster, *A History of French Dramatic Literature in the Seventeenth Century* (Part II, The Period of Corneille, 1635–1651, Baltimore, 1932), I, 133–34.

⁵ Poussin's 'Triumph of Flora' (Fig. 16), like many others among his paintings, is characterized by a mixture of the qualities of both the Renaissance and the Baroque. As is usual in his works, the picture space is organized on the Renaissance principle of division into obvious planes. The first plane is defined by the two reclining figures to the left and by the kneeling woman at the right. It is indicative of Poussin's attitude that all three

figures are disposed in a line that is parallel to the frame. The second plane is occupied by Flora's car and her numerous attendants. Behind them is a group of trees to the left, while to the right is a hill that defines a plane somewhat more distant than that of the trees. In the center, a second hill provides still another stop for the eye. Behind it is a shadowy group of trees that stands outlined against the final plane of the sky. While this side of the picture shows Baroque influence in its mildly diagonal recession, it is plain that an effort is made to organize space in a series of clearly defined parallel planes in keeping with a Renaissance conception of beauty.

The general arrangement of the figures partakes of the qualities of both Renaissance and Baroque. Since most of the figures are moving toward the left, the spectator's eye tends to drift in that direction and out of the picture. This pronounced Baroque tendency is only partly counterbalanced by the disposition of the persons in the left foreground in such a way that they direct the eye back to the right and toward Flora. Even this Renaissance trait has a Baroque flavor, since the eye is led diagonally back to the right and into the depth of the picture, rather than to the right in the same plane, as would have been done in a Renaissance painting.

Light and color are manipulated in a Baroque manner. The trees at the left are rendered in a way that is simultaneously painterly and linear. The outline of the mass of foliage is rendered as a definite line, while the leaves inside this boundary are simply an inchoate splotch of color. This is to be contrasted with the Renaissance practice of outlining each trunk, limb, and leaf with a clear, firm line. In keeping with the technique of the sixteenth century, the chief character is emphasized by a strong color, in the present case the red of her robe. This bright tone, however, is not confined to her but is also used in the clothing of various other persons without respect to their iconographic or formal importance. The figure standing behind the two winged cherubs has a red robe, as do the two women just behind Flora near her right hand. The kneeling woman in the right foreground is also dressed in red, while the armored warrior to her right is clothed partly in the same color. Thus, color is used both rationally to accent the most important person as well as irrationally to emphasize people of much less consequence.

This brief and partial analysis suggests the degree to which Poussin, like Corneille, participated in the ideals of both periods. It goes without saying that he fused these two attitudes into a single composite esthetic ideal that guided his creative work.

⁶ Pérez de Oliva's play is subjected to a detailed analysis of forms similar to that of the present study in Roaten and Sánchez y Escribano, *Wölfflin's Principles*, pp. 55 ff.

⁷ Colbert Searles (ed.), *Les sentiments de l'académie française sur le Cid* (Minneapolis, 1916), p. 111.

⁸ Kohler lends support to this line of argument. 'Mais il faut savoir que c'est dans un cadre baroque plutôt que classique que la France a vécu son "Grand Siècle".' Pierre Kohler, *Histoire de la littérature française* (Paris, 1947), I, 123.

7
Racine, *Phèdre* (1677)[1]

SUMMARY OF PLOT

Phaedra falls in love with her stepson Hippolytus while Theseus, her husband and his father, is away. She is determined to tell no one, but her old nurse Oenone worms the secret out of her. Phaedra tells Hippolytus of her love for him. Hippolytus is horrified and rejects her declaration. Theseus returns soon afterward and Oenone tells him that Hippolytus has been trying to make love to Phaedra. Theseus banishes his son and calls upon Neptune to kill him. Hippolytus is killed as he drives his chariot along the beach. Phaedra confesses to Theseus that Hippolytus was innocent and then dies of poison that she has taken.

PLOT SCHEME

Hippolytus-Phaedra	Theseus-Hippolytus-Phaedra	Hippolytus-Aricia
	Act I	
		i
	ii	
	iii	
	iv	iv
	Act II	
		i
		ii
ii		iii
iii		
iv		
v		
vi		

Hippolytus-Phaedra Theseus-Hippolytus-Phaedra Hippolytus-Aricia

Act III

i
ii

iii
iv
v
vi

Act IV

i
ii
iii
iv
v
vi

Act V

i   i
ii
iii
iv
v
vi
vii

PLOT

In obedience to the Baroque concept of fusion, the plots of *Phèdre* are
interwoven in a complicated fashion. The plot scheme makes this
evident at a glance. There are three motives instead of only one as in
the Renaissance, so that their mere existence enforces the dependence
of each plot on all the others. This would lead one to expect a careful
linking of parts, which in fact does occur. The first scene of the play,
which concerns primarily the principal theme of Theseus, Hippolytus,

and Phaedra, contains a brief hint of the plot that shortly will develop into that of Hippolytus and Aricia (ll. 60–65). After this hint, Hippolytus discusses his own character and that of Theseus for a number of lines and then the conversation reverts to Aricia (ll. 101–38). In line 139, the dialog returns to the chief plot. Scenes i and ii are devoted to the motive of Theseus, Hippolytus, and Phaedra, while scene iv is divided between this theme and that of Aricia. This complex interweaving of plots, so typical of the Baroque esthetic, is repeated in Act II. Scene i concerns Hippolytus and Aricia, while scenes ii and iii continue this motive side by side with that of Hippolytus and Phaedra. The remaining three scenes of this act follow the fortunes of Hippolytus and Phaedra exclusively. Act III continues to deal with the motive of Phaedra and Hippolytus in scenes i and ii, but in iii, with the news that Theseus is alive, there is an abrupt shift back to what is now seen to be the primary line of action, the motive of Theseus, Phaedra, and Hippolytus. Nor is this reappearance of Theseus, sudden though it is, unprepared for. Various unobtrusive remarks scattered through the preceding scenes have kept the audience aware that he may return, although no unequivocal statement to this effect is made. In II, v (ll. 663–66), this exchange takes place between Hippolytus and Phaedra:

Hippolyte
Dieu! Qu'est-ce que j'entends, Madame, oubliez-vous
Que Thésée est mon père, et qu'il est votre époux?
Phèdre
Et sur quoi jugez-vous que j'en perds la mémoire,
Prince?

A few sentences in II, vi (ll. 729–36) serve the same function of reminding the audience of Theseus:

Théramène
Cependant un bruit sourd veut que le roi respire.
On prétend que Thésée a paru dans l'Epire.
Mais moi qui l'y cherchais, Seigneur, je sais trop bien . . .

Hippolyte

N'importe, écoutons tout, et ne négligeons rien.
Examinons ce bruit, remontons à sa source.
S'il ne mérite pas d'interrompre ma course,
Partons; et quelque prix qu'il en puisse coûter,
Mettons le sceptre aux mains dignes de le porter.

It is equally characteristic of the Baroque position that these passages are not frequent enough nor definite enough to lend the feeling of inevitability that would have been sought in a Renaissance play. The sixteenth century, in its pursuit of this characteristic kind of plot development, would have attained it, not by using a greater number of statements to keep the memory of Theseus alive in the audience but rather by avoiding such a necessity. This would have been effected by having only one plot and by keeping it before the spectators at every moment and avoiding the distractions of tributary motives.

With the news of Theseus' return in III, iii, the hitherto separate plot of Hippolytus and Phaedra coalesces with the dominant motive of Theseus, Hippolytus, and Phaedra, and ceases to have an independent existence. In other words, one of the tributary subjects has fused with the leading motive, leaving only that of Hippolytus and Aricia to be joined to the principal line of the story. Act III continues to its end with no further mention of Aricia. Racine, however, is interested in keeping this plot active so that it will be ready to hand when there is need for it later. This is one of the reasons for Hippolytus' confession to his father in IV, ii that he is in love with Aricia. In IV, iv, v, and vi, Aricia is again mentioned. All this prepares, in a quite unobtrusive fashion, for her reappearance on stage in V, i. Throughout the play, the intermingling of the motive of Hippolytus and Aricia with the principal theme has continued. Until the end of V, i, this plot has a relative independence from the leading theme, but, in V, ii, Aricia is on the stage with Theseus for the first time. Here, the two motives are so closely joined that they become one.

The visible symbol of this fusion of major and minor elements into one is the simultaneous presence on stage of a character from each plot who is not common to both. The presence of Hippolytus, who occurs in both, has not served at all to cause nor even to hasten this fusion of themes. But from the moment when Aricia and Theseus come on stage together, the two currents of action are one. From this point on, there is only one theme concerning the four principals—Theseus, Hippolytus, Phaedra, and Aricia. The denouement, when it comes, affects them all with equal emotional impact. At the end, a single motive comes to dominate completely.

During most of the play, the presence of Aricia and Theseus obscures in part the theme of Phaedra and serves to direct attention away from it. Hence, it is only in the last act that it is made clear that her role is the paramount one. The development of the structural forms, proceeding at the same rate as the events of the story, and indeed in necessary co-ordination with them, has gone through all the convolutions typical of the Baroque play and has arrived at the conclusion foreseen and arranged by the playwright from the beginning but carefully concealed from the audience. The Baroque conceives of the drama as an unfolding, 'becoming' action, dynamic in nature and full of detours and surprises, an art form that attains a sufficient clarity but which never aspires to the absolute and unremitting clearness that typifies a play of the Renaissance. This is to be contrasted with the Renaissance assumption that a drama is the setting forth of an action whose full course and denouement the audience can foresee from the beginning. Onto a story borrowed from Euripides, a form characteristic of the seventeenth century has been grafted. The external elements are those of Greek classicism but the spirit of the forms is Baroque.[2] It is this striving for Baroque form that induced Racine to add the secondary plot of Aricia to his play. The single theme of the *Hippolytus* was too austere, too undecorated, and too lacking in complexity to appeal to the late Baroque of Racine's time. Complication was felt by Racine and his contemporaries to be a necessary element of beauty in art; hence, it was introduced in the present case by way of the addition of another part to the story. This points up what few people have denied, that Racine was a truly creative artist and not a mere imitator of models.[3]

L

The above inquiry has recounted at some length the manner in which Racine weaves his themes together. This process insures that the plots shall not appear to be sharply set off from each other, after the manner of the separate scenes of a Renaissance play. The several lines of the story are conceived as parts of one plot, and the esthetic resources at the author's disposal are marshalled and employed in such a way as to make it evident that he conceived the play as a single entity. That is to say, the Baroque author thought in terms of several motives that eventually mingled with the principal theme and were lost in it, while the creative process in the writer of the sixteenth century ran along the lines of a number of separate scenes that never fuse but are held together firmly by a unique plot that stands apart and above all the scenes. There is in *Phèdre* no well defined 'line' of plot but rather a 'mass' of plot material in which three leading motives are perceptible in constant and restless movement in relation to each other.

By employing a repertory of devices evolved by the Baroque for this purpose, Racine in the creation of *Phèdre* avoided an obviously logical development. The feeling of inevitability that is apparent in the Renaissance handling of plot and character is notably absent in the play presently in question. A sustained effort is made to puzzle the audience concerning the course that the unfolding action will follow and, thereby, to maintain the maximum emotional tension. In the opening scene of *Phèdre*, there is no hint of what the plot will be, although the four chief characters participate in this initial scene, Hippolytus by his presence and the other three by being mentioned. It is typical of the Baroque indirect approach to the rendition of dramatic action that the only suggestion of the relationships that these four people will have is misleading. A casual reading or listening to the first scene creates the impression that the story is to concern the love of Hippolytus for Aricia. The Baroque will to the mysterious and uncertain is visible from the beginning. It might be argued that the universal acquaintance with this Greek legend among Racine's auditors gives the story away as soon as the title is known, but this misses the point, which is simply to understand the personal and epochal way in which Racine manipulated plot. Even someone who has read or seen *Phèdre* many times is obligated to re-experience the atmosphere of uncertainty that Racine intends to create by merely hinting at the plot of Hippolytus and Aricia without letting it be known how it will evolve. The feelings to be experienced in the present case are those of mystery and of the curiosity that is consequent upon it. This uncertainty was undreamed of by the Renaissance artist. It is equally impossible to assign these modes of creation to the Classical period of ancient Greece, the opinion of eminent scholars notwithstanding.[4]

The characteristic Baroque discontinuity of action is often embodied in a scene that proceeds to a highly critical point on the verge of a resolution of the situation but is then abruptly cut off without the expected solution. Of such a nature is Act I, scene iii, where Phaedra promises to tell Oenone what is troubling her, but when the disclosure seems imminent there is further delay. The wish to avoid the blunt clarity of earlier dramatic forms is evident.

This same emotion of the mysterious is aimed at in the passage where Phaedra tells Hippolytus of her love for him. A Renaissance writer would have told it no less beautifully, perhaps, but much more directly. Racine drags out the disclosure to considerable length, not from a wish to invent something from nothing but under the impulse of the Baroque wish to be indirect, to focus the audience's attention on an element that serves as a distraction from the matter in hand.[5] The blunt, direct 'Je l'aime' of Corneille's Infanta in referring to Rodrigue indicates the difference in outlook that has supervened since 1636. The same attitudes govern Hippolytus' confession of love for Aricia. The audience perceives its approach long before it arrives but the author still feels it appropriate to hint, to delay, and to have recourse to the intricate and devious methods of the Baroque.

The same uncertainty and tension that characterize these events is apparent in the way in which Act III ends. In III, v, Theseus asks for an explanation of Hippolytus' and Phaedra's mysterious reluctance to welcome him home. The pause at the end of Act III, which follows within a few lines, has the esthetic purpose common to the highly equivocal terminations of Acts I and II. The intent is to leave the audience hanging in mid-air, wondering what the issue of the situation will be. This failure to make a mechanical stop coincide with a concluding cadence in the action is a settled practice of the Baroque that is diametrically opposed to that of the Renaissance. Racine is interested not only in presenting these effects but also in making sure that his audience shall appreciate to the fullest extent the dramatic tension that he has produced. In order to insure this, he has Hippolytus say in III, vi (l. 991), 'Dieux! Que dira le Roi?' As a matter of fact, Hippolytus' entire speech in III, vi, which ends the act, is calculated to drive home the questions raised by this abrupt suspension of action and to increase still more the emotional power contained therein.

The impression should not arise that Racine was capable of these abrupt, intense terminations only at the end of an act. In II, ii, Hippolytus informs Aricia that he is in love with her. Although Aricia has said in II, i that she is in love with Hippolytus, the audience still must feel considerable curiosity concerning her reply to a declaration that she has not foreseen. In a typically Baroque fashion, Racine has Theramenes come in before Aricia can answer. Although the interruption is only a few lines in length and Aricia soon hints that she returns his love (II, iii, ll. 572–76), the determination to turn the attention aside from the chief subject is evident. That is to say, the wish to deviate from the direct line of the evolving plot operates in an individual scene as well as in the manipulation of the larger elements.[6]

The point needs to be made that these devices were not entered into from a frivolous wish to puzzle and then to shock with a cheap theatrical surprise. They constitute one of a series of recourses that were an accepted part of the Baroque attitude toward artistic creation and which go to make up a complex of serious esthetic intentions. To what extent Racine's participation in these intentions was conscious and to what extent unconscious is not nearly so important as is the knowledge that there was a pattern peculiar to the period and that Racine worked under its pervasive guidance.

At the same time that Racine's work gives evidence of a new attitude toward art, it also contains traditional elements inherited from a past epoch. No reference is intended to the Classical period of Greek literature, in line with the opinion already advanced herein that the spirit and forms embodied in Racine's *Phèdre* can be described as essentially late Baroque and Christian. The borrowings from Euripides and others are merely external and do not determine or influence to any appreciable degree the artistic views of which his works are an expression. The traditional survivals referred to are from the Renaissance, the most prominent being the reduction of the elapsed time of the play to a very brief period. In one respect, at least, the Renaissance tradition of the unornamented line of action seems to exert some influence. That is, the usual Baroque deviations from the direct line of the story that are afforded in the Spanish *comedia* by frequent passages of humor and long descriptions are completely missing from *Phèdre*. At the same time, a noticeable departure from the practice in Euripides' *Hippolytus* needs to be remarked upon. In the *Hippolytus*, only the principal actors are given names. The rest are assigned such generic designations as 'Chorus', 'Nurse,' or 'Messenger.' Racine took the trouble to delete the chorus and to give specific names to all the characters. This may be interpreted as a part of the Baroque tendency, which is quite marked in the plastic arts, to make art more intimate than was the case during either the Classical period or the Renaissance.

Another trait of Racine's theater that may be described either as a vestigial survival from the Renaissance or as a borrowing from Classical Greece is the habit of recounting violent action through a messenger rather than having it take place on stage. Without attempting to resolve the question of the origin of such a device as the *récit* of Theramenes, it can be said that it served two purposes, to wit: (1) It followed the ancient tradition of decorum of action on the stage. (2) It avoided the difficult or even impossible problem of putting such a scene on the stage. Guillén de Castro's *Las mocedades del Cid*, which up to the present time has not been accused of any Classical bent, treats two similar scenes of violence in the same way as does Racine. In Castro's play, the duel

between Rodrigo and the Count and the battle between the Christians
and the Moors occur off-stage and are recited to the audience. Hence,
the avoidance of violence on the stage need not be regarded as an echo
of Classicism, even though in both the cases cited it may be quite
possible. It would appear to be somewhat more likely that the given
explanations of decorum and the difficulty in staging are universal or
quasi-universal principles of the theater prior to the invention of the
movie camera. The question of origin, however, is of less moment than
is an accurate description of the esthetic patterns of the period in question and the manner in which these patterns are embodied in specific
works. It must be understood in addition that these remnants of an
earlier time do not function as distinct artistic factors that are separate
from the notably Baroque qualities but rather have been thoroughly
assimilated into the new esthetic.

Under the conditions of mystery concerning plot development, the
relations between the several themes refuse to remain stable. A change
of direction in one plot threatens to have repercussions on all the others,
since all are closely tied together. A few illustrations will suffice. By
II, i, the audience knows that Hippolytus and Aricia are in love with
each other. It would seem, therefore, that they could marry and that
Phaedra would simply have to endure her disappointment, but the
Baroque outlook on art will not permit this. When the emotional
entanglements of Aricia, Hippolytus, and Phaedra become known to
the audience, instead of having recourse to the assumption of the easy
way out that has been suggested, the immediate result is that the questions that arise are, 'How will this turn out? How does Racine intend
to bring about the tragic denouement that is evidently going to follow?'
The wish to mystify by means of a temporary absence of any definite
plot direction is evident. The capital event that gives rise to a feeling of
doubt in *Phèdre* is Theseus' return from Hades. When it is known that
he is still alive, the situation of the other three principals, which was
already uneasy enough, becomes more fluid and shifting than ever.
Into a highly unsettled, three-part equation, a fourth element is cast so
that the turmoil becomes still more pronounced. Nor is it at all possible

to regard this uncertainty and divergence from the single straight line of plot development as an accident. The examples of it are too numerous and they stand out too clearly against the static quality of Renaissance art to allow of this explanation. The drama of Racine evolved according to the same repertory of artistic concepts that animated the gradual transformations of music, painting, sculpture, and architecture during the seventeenth century. That is to say, in the creation of artistic forms, stability no longer appealed to the Baroque, which felt a need for shifting, unstable relationships of the formal constituents.

The element of contrast that is so prominent in the Baroque finds complete expression in the fashion after which the plot of *Phèdre* is managed. Oenone's announcement in III, iii of Theseus' imminent return comes abruptly and without previous preparation. Here, the plot takes a sudden turn in another direction from the one it has been following up to this point. This sharp contrast is prepared intentionally and with such skill that its deliberateness escapes any except a close scrutiny. It is advisable to point out that the previous hints of Theseus' possible return do not constitute a case of divergence from the principle of shock and contrast. Racine in this matter has to deal with two problems. He must keep the plot of Theseus active so that his return will not be wholly unexpected and arbitrary, while at the same time he finds it necessary to suppress these indications sufficiently to be able to draw the maximum shock from his resurrection. The desire for contrast has an equal governance over the manipulation of other events. In III, i, Phaedra sends Oenone to win Hippolytus for her in any way she can. As Phaedra sees her returning, she says (in l. 824), 'On me déteste, on ne t'écoute pas.' This remark, which proceeds so logically from the preceding scenes, firmly convinces the auditors that Oenone brings news of Hippolytus. Therefore, in spite of previous hints that Theseus is alive, the sudden revelation of this bit of news is totally unexpected. The formal pattern here is one of violent contrasts prepared in obedience to a concept of art that was conscious, at least in part.

STYLE

In the style, puns, humor, far-fetched metaphorical conceits, and noticeable departures from a normal word order do not occur, but the principle of contrast finds as full expression as in the plot. In II, i, ll.
449–52, Aricia speaks in these terms of the pleasure she would take in having
Hippolytus in love with her:

> Mais de faire fléchir un courage inflexible,
> De porter la douleur dans une âme insensible,
> D'enchaîner un captif de ses fers étonné,
> Contre un joug qui lui plaît vainement mutiné . . .

It will be noticed that each of the lines quoted consists of two equal
parts and that each half is set off against the idea expressed in the other
half in a paradoxical contradiction. Also, the whole concept dealt with
here, that it is pleasurable to capture and tame an untamed man, is paradoxical in nature. In II, ii, l. 542, Hippolytus declares his love to Aricia
in these terms: 'Présente, je vous fuis; absente, je vous trouve.' Two
opposing ideas are set against each other in a balanced construction that
functions to deliberately call attention to these formal characteristics.
These same observations can be applied with equal force to Hippolytus'
speech immediately after this, in ll. 544–45 and l. 548:

> La lumière du jour, les ombres de la nuit,
> Tout retrace à mes yeux les charmes que j'évite.
> . . . .
> Maintenant je me cherche, et ne me trouve plus.

In II, v (l. 688), Phaedra scolds Hippolytus by saying, 'Tu me
haïssois plus, je ne t'aimois pas moins.' The familiar pattern of antithe-
tical ideas expressed in a balanced, parallel form is as apparent here as in
the example cited above.[7] This use of mutually balanced phrases that
contain the contrasts of opposite ideas is a settled Baroque phenomenon
that is as patent in the Spanish *comedia* of the seventeenth century as it
is in Racine's *Phèdre*. It should be remarked, however, that there seems

to be a conspicuous difference between the handling of the paradox in stylistic forms and ideas in the two countries. This difference can be described in general terms as a less extreme exploitation of opposites in the French theater. In Racine specifically, the paradoxical quality is muted. This seems on the whole to be true of all the more extreme qualities of the Baroque style. It must be said, however, that this relative softening of extremes in *Phèdre* does not vitiate in any way the present line of argument concerning the Baroque style in Racine's play in particular and in the French theater in general. It is in every instance a case of a different kind of Baroque rather than of a Classical style.

A direct, unornamented expression is avoided in favor of a roundabout mode of linguistic representation. Examples are to be had by choosing almost at random, for there are few lines in *Phèdre* that are not the incarnation of indirection. In III, v (ll. 933–34), Hippolytus says:

> Assez dans les forêts mon oisive jeunesse
> Sur de vils ennemis a montré son adresse.

Nothing could be further from the starkly direct style of the Renaissance than these lines, with the rather *précieux* Baroque 'vils ennemis' standing for the wild animals he has killed. The phrase 'a montré son adresse' is equally indirect. This couplet may be regarded as thoroughly representative of the style of *Phèdre*—elevated, roundabout, and filled with substitute expressions that stand for other more everyday phrases, as indicated. Other examples may be noted briefly. In l. 16, Theramenes says, 'Croyez-vous découvrir la trace de ses pas?' In l. 19, he says, 'Et si, lorsqu'avec vous nous tremblons pour ses jours . . .' To use 'la trace de ses pas' to refer to Theseus' whereabouts and 'ses jours' to mean his life is to speak in the indirect terms of Baroque *préciosité*. The same desire to escape from the strictures of ordinary discourse motivates the molding of the expressive forms in l. 379, where Aricia says in reference to Theseus, 'Dit-on quelle aventure a terminé ses jours?' Ismena replies in the same fashion, 'On sème de sa mort d'incroyables discours.' Since the whole play is in a non-realistic style far removed from prose, longer examples than those given lie ready to hand. Phaedra's lengthy declaration of love for Hippolytus in II, v is remote from any relation to realistic discourse. Her speech is fluent and couched in a language far more formal and including more of a deliberate linguistic beauty than would be possible in a woman actually under such emotional stress as Phaedra is in the present instance. Precisely the same observations can be made concerning Hippolytus' avowal of love to Aricia in II, ii.

It is clear enough that Racine did not intend to write prose nor anything near to prose and that his esthetic intentions included nothing related to realism as it was understood by the nineteenth century. He created his works not under the impulse of a scientific interest in recreating an observed, everyday reality, but rather under an urge to create a formal beauty of plot and language in accordance with the ideals of the Baroque. This refutation of the presence in *Phèdre* of what are essentially the artistic intentions of the nineteenth century would be quite superfluous if it were not that much of the criticism that has grown up around Racine has been precisely to this effect.[8] The differences between prose and the language of the present work are so obvious that they hardly need to be mentioned. They are as follows: (1) rhyme; (2) a strongly marked rhythm; (3) an omnipresent preciosity, that is, the preference for the indirect phrase. It is expedient to remark at this juncture that the imputation of preciosity to Racine is not to be interpreted as a mark of contempt but is rather intended as a purely descriptive term. Nor should it be considered an insult to this genius of the first rank that his art seems to give evidence of the forthcoming transformation of the late Baroque into the Rococo. The precious elegance of his language, the use of the tender emotion of love that is so characteristic of his works, and the bland emotional tone that pervades them, all foreshadow the mannered softness of Rococo art forms. In much the same way, the contemporary Molière is an early prophet of the rationalism of the Rococo.[9]

The tone is elevated, as in the Renaissance tragedy, but it is now no longer a case of moving from a majestic tone to a more personal feeling and back again. The dignity of the language moves at every moment in an atmosphere of personal emotion. The elevated style of an earlier time persists but has been so thoroughly acclimated to a new attitude that it is now used to convey an intimacy of feeling that the Renaissance did not make use of in art.

CHARACTERS

Racine conceives and handles his characters in such a way that they partake of the restless ambiguity that is characteristic of the Baroque. Phaedra, in sharp contradistinction to the unwavering devotion to duty that distinguishes Jodelle's Dido, undergoes frequent changes of attitude. Her shifting from love to hate of Hippolytus and back again is typical of the wavering of the Baroque heroine between two opposite lines of conduct. In order to secure revenge for his scorn, she denounces him to Theseus, but his death moves her to retract the accusation before she herself dies. The same indecision can be observed in both Guillén de Castro's *Las mocedades del Cid* and Corneille's *Le Cid*. These emotional transformations are contrary to the Renaissance view of personality as static and unchanging, while they were pleasing and even necessary under the Baroque ideal of art.[10] This mode of approaching a moral problem, in addition to providing the contrasts of perpetually shifting possibilities in the course of the action, lends also the feeling of opposites in emotional values concentrated in the person of a single character. Phaedra, being the chief figure of the play and the center toward which the other characters converge, is naturally the one around whom these oppositions tend to cluster. In IV, vi (ll. 1252 ff), she feels alternately a maniacal fury against Hippolytus and Aricia, and horror at her own sinfulness. The principal ambiguity lies with Phaedra and Hippolytus, between whom, as occurs so often in the seventeenth-century theater, the connection is a double one filled with bizarre contradictions. On the one hand, Phaedra is both mother and mistress; on the other, Hippolytus is son and (potential) lover. In the matter of Phaedra's character, a difference between Garnier's *Hippolyte* and Racine's *Phèdre* is of interest. Garnier places Hippolytus in the center of attention. Racine, in obedience to a new feeling that puts a premium on softness and discounts the harsher aspects of heroism, gives Phaedra the position of first importance in the action. This suggests not merely a personal difference between the two playwrights but an epochal distinction as well between two conceptions of dramatic character.

In the course of the play, Phaedra's primary role becomes evident, but does so only toward the end. The only other figure that enters into serious competition for attention is Hippolytus, who seems to be of equal prominence with Phaedra until the last act. After the account of Hippolytus' death by Theramenes (V, vi), Phaedra is left in the high relief toward which the formal arrangements have tended from the beginning but which becomes evident only in the concluding scenes. The precise nature of this mode of conceiving characters can be more completely understood if it is compared on the one hand with the Renaissance practice of keeping the principal figure or figures permanently in the center of attention, and on the other with the habit of the Spanish *comedia* of playing up the tributary characters even more than is done in *Phèdre*.

The secondary personages are no longer the retiring figures of the Renaissance theater. Oenone, instead of keeping always in the background, now and then shows an individualized personality; her anger and her determination to kill herself if Phaedra dies constitute such an approach to the rendition of personality. In I, iii (ll. 227–30), Oenone says:

> Mourez donc, et gardez un silence inhumain;
> Mais pour fermer vos yeux cherchez une autre main.
> Quoiqu'il vous reste à peine une foible lumière,
> Mon âme chez les morts descendra la première.

The extreme differences between Phaedra and Aricia offer another pertinent instance of the new position in the depiction of human nature. Phaedra is resolute and even fierce at times; her powerful will and her certainty of what she wants are fitted to her maturity and indicate distinctly the heroic role that Racine had in mind for her. Aricia, who is only a girl, has a tender charm and gentleness that are in keeping with her youthfulness and the sweetly passive part that she is expected to take. The point to be made here is that Aricia, a secondary personage, has a fully developed temperament that distinguishes her sharply from Phaedra. The distinction between this technique and that of the Renaissance is apparent, if the colorlessness of Dido's sister Bartia in Jodelle's *Didon* is recalled. Along with this reference to the sixteenth-century theater, it is apropos to compare with Racine's procedure in these matters the even clearer definition of such minor figures as Clarín in Calderón's *La vida es sueño*. The relative conservatism in this respect, which has already been remarked on in regard to the forms of *Le Cid*, persists into Racine's work of a generation later.

It is equally indicative of a Baroque attitude that each of the characters is related to several personages rather than to one only. Aricia, who does not figure in the leading plot, is related not merely to Hippolytus but also to Theseus and, by implication, to Phaedra. Oenone does not limit herself to talking with her mistress but plays a part of some importance as a go-between with Hippolytus and as an informer to Theseus. Theseus' close personal connection with Phaedra, Hippolytus, and Aricia is demonstrated in his conversations with each of them. Hippolytus, who is himself secondary to Phaedra, is related to Phaedra, Aricia, and Theseus, as well as to Oenone. At the end, however, all these complex relationships are minimized in order to allow Phaedra to stand out sharply against the confused background that they provide. In the Renaissance theater, these complicated interconnections of many characters would have been avoided in favor of two dominant figures, each with his train of secondary actors related to him alone. To the Baroque of Racine's time, these simple relations of separate parts are no longer desirable and a greater complexity is preferred.

A consideration of the facts and interpretations that have been set forth lead to a number of pertinent conclusions concerning *Phèdre*, which in turn lead to some equally relevant inferences in regard to various broader critical problems. They may be stated as follows: *Phèdre* is not a Classical work. It pertains rather to the late Baroque school,[11] with isolated elements that anticipate the Rococo and others that are reminiscent of the Renaissance. There are also echoes of the Greek Classical period in the choice of the subject, which nevertheless fails to exercise any perceptible influence upon the esthetic ideals of this play. The present analysis and its findings concerning one of Racine's masterpieces casts a serious doubt on the validity of the conventional criticism relating to the rest of his plays and indeed on all the safe and sane interpretations of the literature of seventeenth-century France. This points up the urgent need for the permanent exile of nineteenth-century positivism from the repertory of concepts concerning literary criticism. Consequent upon this need is the pressing necessity of developing a critical apparatus capable of yielding valid results. This demand has been met with great capability in a small number of isolated cases, which are still far from exerting sufficient corrective influence to secure the establishment of a school of criticism that is devoted to the study of literature as an art rather than as an exercise in the indiscriminate collection of data and the application to a past period of divers esthetic concepts that are largely anachronistic.

Notes

[1] The text used is as follows: Jean Racine, *Oeuvres de J. Racine*, ed. Paul Mesnard ('Les grands écrivains de la France,' Paris, 1865), III, 243–397. Subsequent references to *Phèdre* are from this edition and will be indicated only by citing the act, scene, or lines as the case may be.

[2] 'This harmonizing of civilizations in Racine's *Phèdre*, Greek, Christian, and French, is the pinnacle of Classicism.' (William A. Nitze and E. Preston Dargan, *A History of French Literature*, 3rd ed. [New York, 1938], p. 321.) The first part of this pronouncement, being a question of iconography, may be left to one side for the purposes of the present study. To call *Phèdre* the pinnacle of Classicism, however, is to confuse seventeenth-century French art with that of ancient Greece and mistake the external for the essence.

[3] Nitze and Dargan attempt to make Racine into both creative artist and imitator at once. 'It is Racine's knowledge of Greek, in which he is unique among *les grands classiques*, that accounts for the creative quality of his style.' (Nitze and Dargan, *French Literature*, p. 321.) In this, there appears the passion of the nineteenth century for explaining everything, even a phenomenon so intensely personal and epochal as Racine's style, in terms of scientific cause and effect. The statement may be reduced to a formula something after this nature: 'Greek literature (cause) produces Racine's style (effect).' It should be clear that the origins of any work of art must be sought in the artist and in the contemporary

culture of which he is a part. Explanations of cause and effect obscure the problem instead of illuminating it.

⁴ 'In all respects, Racine's plays had the added advantage of obeying the Classical rules as outlined by d'Aubignac and Boileau.' (Nitze and Dargan, *French Literature*, pp. 320–21.)

'. . . grâce au grec qu'on lui avait enseigné à Port-Royal, il savait où trouver des modèles de ce qui manquait à la tragédie française.' (Eugène Lintilhac, *Précis historique et critique de la littérature française*, 2nd ed. [Paris, 1895], II, 44.)

⁵ 'It is extraordinary, as in the case of *Bérénice*, how he [Racine] discerns the drama that lurks in a few words of some ancient poet or historian.' (Nitze and Dargan, *French Literature*, p. 320.) Behind this statement lies the positivistic assumption that the brief remark of the ancient poet or historian functions as the source (i.e., the cause) of a play (the effect). Such an assumption pertains to the nineteenth-century attitude toward art. There exists no such cause and effect relation and therefore no reason for astonishment.

⁶ '. . . sa [Racine's] tragédie est une suite de coups de théâtre et de révolutions . . . l'objet est toujours une résolution à prendre, qui est prise, rejetée, reprise, autant de fois que s'excercent l'impulsion ou l'inhibition . . .' (Lanson, *Littérature française*, p. 543.)

Lanson perceives now and then a quality of the Baroque theater, as he does here. But because he approaches the seventeenth century with categories drawn from the nineteenth century, he fails to fit these isolated perceptions into a coherent view of Baroque art.

⁷ 'Cette élégance [of Racine's style] consiste essentiellement dans un choix harmonieux des mots, si éloigné du cliquetis des antithèses . . .' (Lintilhac, *Précis historique*, II, 47.) Even the brief analysis engaged in here indicates clearly enough the deliberate and frequent use that Racine made of antithesis. The expression concerning the 'choix harmonieux des mots' is vague and meaningless because it points out a stylistic ideal toward which many writers of many different periods have labored. It fails to lead to an understanding of Racine because it neglects to locate him in a pattern peculiar to a single period of art history or to postulate a series of convincing universal principles of criticism capable of leading to an understanding of Racine's drama as art. It may be remarked in passing that the orientation of the present volume toward an epochal view of art history should not be construed as a denial of the possibility of discovering these general characteristics. Cleanth Brooks has presented in his *The Well-Wrought Urn* a convincing defense of the use of universal standards in judging literature.

The strictures levied herein against a number of the standard critical works in French literature should not be construed as an attempt to belittle them for the pleasure there is in it, for that would have a merely negative pedagogical value. The usual American student, having been assiduously instructed in a critical system whose principles are those of materialism, positivism, and scientific realism, inevitably falls into the same fallacy as these distinguished scholars. The correction of these outmoded attitudes becomes an intellectual necessity, for, otherwise, criticism would remain static and sterile.

⁸ 'Le style [of Racine] est pareil; simple et naturel avant tout, juste, précis, intense, rasant la prose, comme disait Sainte-Beuve . . . le style se rabat, tout près de la prose, dans l'indication exacte des faits.' (Lanson, *Littérature française*, pp. 545, 551.)

⁹ For a discussion of Molière's *Don Juan* as an early manifestation of the Rococo, see Joaquín Casalduero, 'Contribución al estudio del tema de Don Juan en el teatro español,' *Smith College Studies in Modern Languages*, XIX (April, July 1938), pp. 59–63.

¹⁰ 'L'intéret [in Racine's plays] étant soutenu jusqu'au bout par ce jeu de passions, il n'avait plus à s'embarrasser d'incidents plus ou moins surprenants, de caractères plus ou moins extraordinaires.' (Lintilhac, *Précis historique*, II, 46.) The evidence cited from *Phèdre*

leads to quite the opposite conclusion insofar as the 'incidents plus ou moins surprenants' are concerned. As for the 'caractères plus ou moins extraordinaires,' it would be difficult to recall a literary character less ordinary than Phaedra or a situation more removed from the everyday than that in which she finds herself involved. The quotation from Lintilhac furnishes another instance of the habit, so firmly settled in such a large number of critics, of reading into the literature of a past period their own preconceptions of what literature should be. In this case, the ideals of nineteenth-century realism are imposed on the Baroque theater of France.

[11] The following remark by Thierry Maulnier gives some idea of the direction in which the current of French criticism is setting of late. 'Je suis enclin à vous donner raison sur plus d'un point, et particulièrement quand vous [André Malraux] dites: "*Phèdre* est un grand poème baroque. Il me fait bien moins penser à l'ordre de Poussin qu'a Monteverdi, dont il partage les moments de déchirante noblesse qui surgissent d'une sorte de confusion nocturne . . ." ' (*Le Figaro littéraire*, 19 mars 1955, p. 3, article by Thierry Maulnier.)

Conclusion

The small number of plays that have been studied herein and the consequent slightness of evidence regarding the general trends of the total body of serious dramatic works in France during the periods in question, all dictate that any conclusions that are reached shall remain tentative until further work has been done. With this reservation, it is possible to state that the present investigation has indicated the feasibility of formal analysis in the drama. It also appears reasonable to suggest that it has demonstrated the possibility of distinguishing between two epochs in the theater on the basis of such an analysis. The practicability of extending a study of this nature to other literary genres is also indicated, although this would need to be done with due care for the proper adjustments made necessary by passing from the drama to another literary form. The esthetic chronology that has been deduced from this investigation can be described in the following terms: In the early part of the sixteenth century, the theater turned from the medieval plays to a Renaissance style, which moved gradually through a transitional stage into the Baroque of the seventeenth century and on into the Rococo at the end of that century (i.e. about 1675–1700). This chronology, if valid, brings the French theater into line with that of Spain as well as with music and the plastic arts throughout Europe, all of which demonstrably followed much the same pattern as the one that has been described. In view of the evidence that has been presented, all the presumptions run to the effect that the French drama did follow this chronological succession. Hence, it can be said that the narrow and rigorous national limitations that are implied in the usual compartmentalized treatment of the French theater of the seventeenth century did not in reality exist in literature, just as they did not subsist in music and the plastic arts. Whether it be a question of Renaissance or Baroque, each of these large artistic movements constituted in all cases and in every sense an international European artistic ideal that underwent the influence of numerous local and individual vagaries of taste but which did not diverge markedly from the epochal pattern.

Corneille, to take a prominent example, was not the great innovator that he is generally considered to be. As all artists must do, he worked with a traditional heritage which he remolded to a certain degree and to which he added his own distinctive contribution. There was in his case no abrupt break with the past; on the contrary, he formed an integral part of the continuous stream of artistic transformation that began before his work and continued after it. His writings cannot be considered an awesome monument of originality that must be approached in the reverential spirit that is indicated in the prescribed formula of *noli me tangere.* A blind adulation even of such eminent artists as Corneille and Racine does no service either to the man or to his works. The imperative necessity is not an undiscriminating praise but rather an understanding of the work of art as a whole.

These same remarks apply in the opposite sense but with equal force to the Renaissance theater. It is of no profit to denigrate the dramatic works of this period as dull and lacking in action. It is true enough that a sixteenth-century play at present gives rise to an almost universal boredom and it is hardly possible to read one for pleasure. This may be and probably is to be attributed to the inferior talent of the playwrights of the time. If this consideration be set aside, however, it is apparent that the artistic principles of the theater of the sixteenth century are sufficiently removed from those of the present day to insure that the modern reader will overlook or misunderstand them and that in any case he is unable to sympathize with them. The Baroque drama was created on the basis of principles that are still largely active in the theater of the twentieth century and they can therefore be read or seen with a relatively unimpaired sympathy and artistic perception. This points up the first problem of the critic in dealing with the Renaissance and the Baroque, as indeed with any period of art history, which is to arrive at a comprehension of their art works by penetrating in each case to the animating ideal of beauty.

Bibliography

Baïf, Lazare de. *Tragédie de Sophocle intitulée Electra*. Paris, 1537.

Bénézit, Emmanuel, ed. *Dictionnaire critique et documentaire des peintres, sculpteurs, dessinateurs et graveurs de tous les temps et de tous les pays*. 3 vols. Paris, 1924–26.

Buffum, Imbrie. *Agrippa d'Aubigné's 'Les tragiques,' a Study of the Baroque Style in Poetry*. Yale University, 1951.

Casalduero, Joaquín. 'Contribución al estudio del tema de Don Juan en el teatro español,' *Smith College Studies in Modern Languages*, XIX (April, July 1938).

Corneille, Pierre. *Oeuvres de P. Corneille*, edited by Ch. Marty-Laveaux. 'Les grands écrivains de la France', Vol. III. Paris, 1862.

Théâtre complet de Corneille, edited by Pierre Lièvre. n.p., n.d.

Dabney, Lancaster Eugene. *French Dramatic Literature in the Reign of Henri IV; a Study of the Extant Plays Composed in French Between 1589 and 1610*. Austin, Texas, 1952.

Garnier, Robert. *Oeuvres complètes (théâtre et poésies) de Robert Garnier*, edited by Lucien Pinvert. Paris, 1923.

Gracián y Morales, Baltasar. *Agudeza y arte de ingenio*. 'Biblioteca de filósofos españoles,' directed by Eduardo Ovejero y Maury. Madrid, 1929.

Hardy, Alexandre. *Le théâtre d'Alexandre Hardy parisien*, edited by E. Stengel. 5 vols. Marburg, 1884.

Kohler, Pierre. *Histoire de la littérature française*. Vol. I. Lausanne, 1947.

Lancaster, H. C. 'A History of French Dramatic Literature in the Seventeenth Century.' Part II *The Period of Corneille, 1635–1651*, Vol. I. Baltimore, 1932.

Lanson, Gustave. *Histoire de la littérature française*. 14th edition. Paris, 1920.

Lebègue, Raymond. *La tragédie française de la renaissance*. Brussels, 1944.

Lintilhac, Eugène. *Précis historique et critique de la littérature française*. 2nd edition. 2 vols. Paris, 1895.

Murray, Gilbert. *Euripides and His Age*. New York, 1913.

Nitze, William A., and Dargan, E. Preston. *A History of French Literature*. 3rd edition. New York, 1938.

Racine, Jean. *Oeuvres de J. Racine*, edited by Paul Mesnard. 'Les grands écrivains de la France,' Vol. III. Paris, 1865.

Rigal, Eugène. *Alexandre Hardy et le théâtre français*. Paris, 1889.

Roaten, Darnell, and F. Sánchez y Escribano. *Wölfflin's Principles in Spanish Drama:* 1500–1700. New York, 1952.

Searles, Colbert, ed. *Les sentiments de l'Académie française sur le Cid*. Minneapolis, 1916.

Sturel, René. 'Essai sur les traductions du théâtre grec en français avant 1550,' *Revue d'histoire littéraire de la France*, XX (1913), pp. 269–96.

Talagrand, Jacques. Article in *Le Figaro littéraire*, le 19 mars, 1955, p. 3.

Thieme, Ulrich, and Becker, Felix, eds. *Allgemeines Lexikon der bildenden Künstler von der Antike bis zur Gegenwart*. 37 vols. Leipzig, 1907–50.

Thierry Maulnier, pseudonym. *See* Talagrand, Jacques.

Williamson, George C., ed. *Bryan's Dictionary of Painters and Engravers*. New edition, revised and enlarged. 5 vols. New York, 1903–1905.